David Hardaker is an experienced Walkley Award–winning investigative journalist who has worked for *Four Corners*, *7.30*, *Foreign Correspondent* and *60 Minutes*. As Investigations Editor at *Crikey* he broke a number of major stories on Hillsong Church.

DAVID HARDAKER

MINE IS THE KINGDOM

*The rise and fall of Brian Houston and
the Hillsong Church*

ALLEN&UNWIN
SYDNEY·MELBOURNE·AUCKLAND·LONDON

Some names and identifying details have been changed to protect the privacy of individuals.

First published in 2024

Allen & Unwin
Cammeraygal Country
83 Alexander Street
Crows Nest NSW 2065
Australia
Phone: (61 2) 8425 0100
Email: info@allenandunwin.com
Web: www.allenandunwin.com

Allen & Unwin acknowledges the Traditional Owners of the Country on which we live and work. We pay our respects to all Aboriginal and Torres Strait Islander Elders, past and present.

 A catalogue record for this book is available from the National Library of Australia

ISBN 978 1 76106 912 3

Set in 11.5/18 pt Sabon LT Pro by Midland Typesetters, Australia
Printed and bound in Australia by the Opus Group

10 9 8 7 6 5 4 3 2 1

The paper in this book is FSC® certified. FSC® promotes environmentally responsible, socially beneficial and economically viable management of the world's forests.

CONTENTS

INTRODUCTION

The Summit of Power

Brian Houston had never made any secret of what he wanted: world domination.

Not for himself, mind, but for the Lord Jesus. When the family business is about saving souls, relentless expansion is what it's all about.

And so it was on this night in July 2019. Houston, the global pastor of the mighty church that was his creation, commanded a Sydney stage and the rapturous attention of 20,000 followers, who had travelled from across the continent and from foreign lands to hear his words.

Was it preaching? Call it the Brian Houston Experience. Nights like these were more a showcase of power. Speaking from a raised dais at the centre of an Olympic-sized auditorium, with giant images of himself projected onto the panels of a circular dome above him, he moved restlessly from one side of the stage to the other.

Houston was speaking of the rain that was coming to quench the parched lands of the nation and, of course, its soul. On other occasions he had filled his followers with the hope that they, too, could be kings and queens, no matter how small their lives might feel. Lives could be redeemed. The lost could find their way home. Miracles could happen to the most ordinary of folk.

Houston had recognised early in his ever-rising career that there was a market for soul-saving in the arid suburbs of Australia and elsewhere in the cities of the West. For lives starved of meaning and looking for purpose, Houston's Hillsong provided a ready solution. That was what brought them out in droves.

Now in his sixties, he had the purpose and energy of a man half his age. Some are diminished by the limelight, but not Brian Houston. On the contrary, Houston stalked around his stage. He pivoted. He pointed. At one moment he descended the stage to cuddle a baby.

His forehead was, magically, wrinkle-free. His teeth perfect. His hair combed back and gelled in place. It didn't look natural— and it probably wasn't. He wore a white, open-necked shirt and tan-leather loafers, with a matching kerchief sprouting from the pocket of a blue jacket—the very picture of relaxed West Coast wealth. Be like him and you too will prosper.

Surely it was God who had given Houston this voice—deep and resonant, projecting the strength and power the meek could only crave. He knew what he had and he used it. He built waves of cresting intensity, sweeping up the shiny-faced seekers of truth who sat before him.

———

In a country where Christianity has been on a steady decline, Pentecostalism has enjoyed a disproportionately high profile, due in great part to Brian Houston and Hillsong.

On this particular night he summoned up to the stage Australia's prime minister, Scott Morrison, the first Pentecostal Christian to lead the nation—indeed, the first Pentecostal Christian to lead any nation. Morrison and his wife, Jenny, received a heroes' welcome as they made their way through the throng to join Brian Houston at centre stage.

Two months earlier, Morrison had won the 2019 general election—a result he had hailed as a 'miracle'. He would later recount how he was spurred on during the dark days of the election campaign by what he saw as messages from God to keep on going.

'We love Jesus,' Morrison proclaimed to the crowd, amid whoops of joy. 'Anyone else feel that way?' More wild applause.

The two men—the pastor and the politician—prayed on stage together. Both of them, at this moment, were at the peak of their powers. Could anyone present have predicted that, within three years, the miraculous prime minister would suffer a humiliating defeat and lose his job, and the master pastor would suffer an equally humiliating defeat at the hands of his followers?

1
GENESIS

Zero to Hero

Brian Houston is a man who came to us from the world of miracles and wonders, and he has quite a story to tell.

It all began in small-town New Zealand. As the second generation of the Houston dynasty, Brian inherited his father's name as a leading New Zealand preacher, but not much in the way of wealth. It's a story he has told in sermons praising God's plan.

'I grew up in a country of three million people, seventy million sheep,' he told his followers at the peak of his powers in 2017. 'I grew up in a state-owned house. True story, I grew up in a state-owned house—1197 Taita Drive, Lower Hutt, New Zealand. My phone number was 67139—back in those days, that was only five numbers. That's how small my world was.'

Brian was one of five Houston kids. As a teenager, he was the shy son, the one who played drums in his dad's church. He swept floors in the local Griffin's biscuit factory at night. He attended Bible college and was so lacking in confidence that he would run from the room rather than stand and speak in front of others. He also held down a job as a window cleaner, and at one time was a soft-drink salesman.

The best thing that ever happened to him was meeting Roberta, aka Bobbie. Brian was nineteen; Bobbie was sixteen, going on seventeen, and worked as a secretary at a pharmaceutical company. She had already encountered God and was attending a Christian convention, where she spotted the son of New Zealand's leading Pentecostal preacher in the crowd on a beach in Tauranga.

Brian was a gangly, kind-of-cute guy, and he loved God. When he met Bobbie, he thought all his Christmases had come at once. Four years later they were married.

The Houston narrative of zero to hero describes what can happen if you believe in God and work hard. If you have a go, you get a go. It also helps if your father is one of the most powerful and revered figures in New Zealand's Pentecostal movement, as Frank Houston was. And it helps even more if you are dealing in the exotic realms of Pentecostalism—a Christian denomination which has historically been a magnet for charlatans and hucksters.

———

Pentecostal megachurches tend to be father-and-son businesses in which stage performance is the secret to success. In that sense, the Houstons are a showbiz family. It helps that they have fabulous material to work with.

In the Pentecostal world, the extraordinary reigns. It is a place full of demons, where Satan is real, and where every day a fierce supernatural war is waged between God and the Devil. Even to many religious folk, this is an alien vision. But it is a marketer's dream.

Pentecostalism is young, fresh, energetic. It is wholly different from the old 'purple' denominations, which for many years have struggled to draw crowds. As those within the movement say, God is 'better felt than telt'. The phrase sums up the magic allure of Pentecostalism: you *feel* it, as opposed to talking about it (or being told about it—*telt*—as the old Scottish dialect has it).

Pentecostalists believe that theirs is religion as it should be done—and, indeed, as it was meant to be done. That is spelled out in the story of the Feast of Pentecost—an Old Testament feast, also known as the Feast of Weeks, because it happened seven weeks after the Jewish feast of Passover.

The number seven is key. Seven has its own divine properties. Seven weeks—it is like a week of weeks. It is seven times seven days. The Pentecost comes on day fifty, with a derivation tracking back to the Greek word 'pentekostos' meaning fiftieth.

The Old Testament's feast of Pentecost is significant in the New Testament, too: it was on this day that the Holy Spirit descended upon the apostles of Jesus Christ. The assembled began to speak in tongues—a miraculous event in itself. As the fifth book of the New Testament, the Acts of the Apostles, records it, 'suddenly from heaven there came a sound like the rush of a violent wind', and it filled the entire house, where more than 100 men were sitting:

Divided tongues, as of fire, appeared among them, and a tongue rested on each of them. All of them were filled with the Holy Spirit and began to speak in other languages, as the Spirit gave them ability.

Now there were devout Jews from every people under heaven living in Jerusalem. And at this sound the crowd gathered and was bewildered, because each one heard them speaking in the native language of each.

Amazed and astonished, they asked, 'Are not all these who are speaking Galileans? And how is it that we hear, each of us, in our own native language?'

This would be a boon for missionary work, because it made it possible to convey the word of God without needing to learn other languages. Speaking in tongues would mean that every Christian could participate in miraculous ministry and see God heal people, and miracles happen, and demons cast out.

Today's Pentecostalists see themselves as restoring the practices of the Pentecost and the attendant miracles of God, as described in the Acts of the Apostles. The history of modern Pentecostalism is replete with stories of miracles and unexplained events, and of instances of the Holy Spirit arriving unbidden.

Australian accounts from the early 1900s record the story of a Perth woman who found herself 'laughing heartily' and nearly 'sinking to the ground as she began speaking in tongues' while walking home from a Pentecostal meeting.

One man spoke of seeing an angel hovering over his bed as he lay dying of diphtheria. He 'felt the wind over his face', and after that was said to have recovered quickly.

A young girl was healed of toothache by the laying on of hands, while her brother, who was dying in hospital from typhoid and pneumonia, staged a miracle recovery at the very time prayers were being offered at a gospel hall.

A poor family with no money for food found that a grey and white bird flew down and perched in front of them with a ten-shilling note in its beak.

Pentecostal Christians also subscribe to end-of-days concepts, which separate them from traditional religious beliefs. Perhaps the best known of these is the Rapture, the event when true Christian believers will be taken up from Earth to meet Christ, in order to return with Him at His second coming. These beliefs are drawn from various interpretations of verses handpicked from the books of the Bible, authored at different times and taken to mean this.

The Rapture will occur during the time of the 'pre-tribulation'. This is the belief that the Christian age will end with a time of intense tribulation, usually thought to be of seven years' duration, during which the wrath of God will be poured out on the Earth, followed by the return of Christ.

A religion so rich in supernatural signs and exotic manifestations, such as speaking in tongues, has attracted its share of colourful characters. An early overseas visitor to Australia's shores was the fabulously named Smith Wigglesworth, the son of a poor rural British family, who became a born-again Christian at the age of eight and later trained to be a plumber. But Wigglesworth's true calling was to be an evangelist around the world.

He believed healing came through faith. While this belief was not notable in itself, he distinguished himself by his method. He would hit the person he was healing, as a demonstration of faith in God: God would cause it to be healing rather than harmful. And Wigglesworth wowed believers in Australia when he prophesied that Australia would be home to a mighty revival, with God using Australia 'to impact the nations'.

Pentecostalism has also been fertile ground over the years for larger-than-life American preachers. Among the most famous is the charismatic evangelist Oral Roberts, who set up the Oral Roberts Organisation in Australia in the mid-1950s. Its purpose was to take the message far and wide, with tent meetings and a so-called 'miracle film', praying for the sick and presenting the gospel.

Oral Roberts' story includes one of those 'tall tales but true' moments, when God allegedly chose him to preach. At age 29, Roberts said, he picked up his Bible and it fell open at the Third Letter of John, verse 2: 'I wish above all things that thou mayest prosper and be in health, even as thy soul prospereth.' The next day he bought a Buick and God appeared, directing him to heal the sick. Roberts promptly set off on evangelistic and faith-healing drives around the United States and around the world, claiming that he could raise the dead.

Such is the religious heritage of the Houstons—a version of Pentecostal religion which could have been designed for entrepreneurs.

As the Houston story would show, all things were possible if you had the spirit to spread the word of Jesus Christ. If you had a go you would certainly get a go—and a God-given go at that.

The very basis of the denomination was that its believers should use their position to gain yet more followers for the movement. Speaking in tongues, a form of vocalising that transcended individual languages, was an essential part of that. Miracles, too, transcended cultures and systems of logic.

If God placed you in a position of power then you should use that to bring more believers to the cause. The wealthy would book a place in heaven by using their money to bring more souls to Jesus Christ.

Celebrities could use their fame to make faith sexy.

The Houstons would start small and end up very big indeed, with believers who ticked all the boxes of influence. They included rock stars, the uber-wealthy of business and a national political leader in Australian prime minister, Scott Morrison.

They in turn would work to populate the pillars of society with yet more believers.

In the name of bringing souls to Jesus, the religion of Frank and Brian Houston would turn traditional religious values on their head by celebrating power, wealth and prestige.

The mighty oak, of course, starts from a tiny acorn. In the case of the Houstons it all began in rural New Zealand where the family lived alongside the poor and struggling.

In short the Houstons knew very well what it meant to be meek. But it wouldn't last long, as Frank Houston soon became New Zealand's legendary showman pastor.

The Father

Frank Houston's illustrious—and wicked—career as a saviour of souls began in the hard-scrabble backblocks of 1950s rural New Zealand. He had begun his life of religious 'service' with the Salvation Army at age eighteen, when he'd helped run an Army boys' home in the town of Temuka, on New Zealand's South Island. He then left the staid Baptist Church and found his home in the flashier end of evangelical Christianity, a place where no one was too worried about your theological qualifications—as long as you had the gift of the gab, which Frank assuredly did.

Frank Houston was an officer with the Salvation Army when he met his wife, Hazel, who was also in the Salvos. Brian came along in 1954. He was the third of five Houston children. With three girls and two boys, there was only one other son vying as a contender to inherit the family business. But Brian's brother, Graeme, had little interest in Pentecostalism. He later got away from the family to live in a flat with his long-haired mates, where he could listen to rock music without his mother 'praying for the Lord to stop it', as Hazel remembered it. This meant Brian would be the male heir, and by all accounts Frank treated him like a little messiah.

There was nothing easy about life in rural New Zealand at this time. The Houstons knew poverty, struggling to make ends meet on a paltry Salvation Army salary. Whether it was the pressure of finances or something else, Frank suffered breakdown after breakdown, even as Brian was in nappies. Hazel later recalled the day Frank was brought home zombie-like after going missing for hours, helped to the front door by two Salvation

Army men. 'He stared vacantly at me,' she later recounted. 'The truth hit me hard: Frank was an emotional and mental wreck.' She begged God for answers. The doctors apparently called it 'hysterical amnesia'.

Frank ultimately found his metier when he drifted into the more showy and—literally—hands-on realm of Pentecostal preaching. The slight, bespectacled preacher could flick the switch to fire-and-brimstone when the moral position demanded it.

By 1959 he was in charge of the Lower Hutt Assemblies of God, near Wellington. The then 37-year-old had a vision, as recorded by Hazel in a church pamphlet called '100 Men': 'It began the day God spoke through a vision. A field of ripe cocksfoot [a type of grass] rippled in the wind. As Frank Houston watched it, it appeared to become a vast crowd of people—people to be reached with the Gospel.' Prophetic indeed.

The church grew rapidly. It opened 'outreach' branches in neighbouring areas. Frank established the Christian Life Bible College, which attracted students from around the globe. Hazel became the college's first matron.

A congregant from this time remembers Frank Houston's practice of dressing up as an old lady and initiating play-fights with boys in their teens and younger in a room at the Lower Hutt church complex.

As he grew in influence, Frank would sometimes be away from the family for weeks at a time, leaving Hazel at home as he spread the word of Jesus to remote parts of New Zealand. Regularly out of contact with home, he was a free agent, which suited him just fine.

Pastor Frank adopted the style of the Latter Rain movement, a revivalist offshoot of a splinter group within the Pentecostal church. The 'latter rain' refers to the last rains poured down from God, marking the end of the Jewish harvest. The leaders of the movement promoted the idea that, as the end of the age approached, the manifested sons of God would appear in the church. They would be empowered with supernatural gifts and be able to perform miracles comparable to those carried out by Jesus Christ, as recorded in the New Testament.

Frank Houston's style was a drawcard for the lost and vulnerable. One of those was a teenager called Peter Fowler, who came to know the pastor as a 'great teacher and a healer'. Frank taught the boy how to do a perfect Windsor knot for his tie. He was also happy to have the teenager along for the long drives as he toured New Zealand.

Peter Fowler remembers a man who was hailed by adoring followers wherever he travelled: 'He knew how to work the crowd. And he knew how to give them what they wanted. He would get people up on their feet, singing and dancing and clapping and doing crazy things. And he made a big show out of it.

'He had the so-called gifts of the Holy Spirit, which meant he could lay his hands on people who were sick and they would be healed. And he liked to make that as entertaining as possible. You know, there's ways of doing it gently and quietly, but he wanted to get maximum value out of it. So when he applied his palm to someone's head to transmit the Holy Spirit, he made sure everybody fell back. And he had people catching them.'

The practice described by Fowler is known as being 'slain in the spirit'; it involves falling over under the power of the spirit. Others witnessed the miracle of legs being lengthened, typical of the outlandish flourishes that lent a circus touch to the business of church. Frank also made the blind see again: 'I rebuke this spirit of blindness in Jesus' name,' he would command, with the confidence of divine authority.

Frank the showman was packing in the crowds all over New Zealand with his version of Pentecostal Christianity, which of course came direct from the United States. Whether or not the miracles in his church were real was apparently beside the point. Parishioners flocked in their thousands to his little Assemblies of God church near Wellington.

The Latter Rain movement was big and theatrical, and it allowed Frank Houston to charm and entertain a crowd. It was also, as Peter Fowler came to conclude, the perfect business model: 'Well, if they weren't healed, of course, it was their fault, because they didn't believe enough. So it was their faith that was at fault, not Frank Houston.'

The sheer numbers Houston garnered propelled him to the very top of New Zealand's Assemblies of God movement, where he ruled for twelve years, until 1977, as General Superintendent, effectively a law unto himself. But new fields beckoned.

The Lord had a plan. It came to Pastor Frank in the early morning hours one day, when he was awakened by the voice of God speaking through his spirit. Hazel later documented the moment in her account of Frank's extraordinary achievements.

'Take your Bible and read Isaiah 54,' the voice had commanded.

It was here that the blueprint emerged, not just for Frank but for the entire Houston dynasty. Isaiah 54 revealed what must be done:

Enlarge the place of your tent and stretch out the curtain of your dwellings. Spare not. Lengthen thy cords and strengthen your pegs, for you will spread abroad to the right hand and to the left.

And thy descendants will possess nations and they will resettle the desolate cities. Fear not for you will not be put to shame. Neither feel humiliated for you will not be disgraced.

'What is this, Lord? What are you saying?' the awe-struck pastor had prayed to know.

It was then that a picture of Sydney, Australia, came before him.

'Sydney. Open a centre in Sydney,' the voice said.

It was exactly what Frank had wanted to hear. The preacher's heart leapt.

The Houston family had begun to travel across the Tasman Sea to Australia from 1970, with young Brian occasionally joining his father on his forays. Now Frank Houston had God's go-ahead.

From little New Zealand, he stepped out to the Great South Land of the Holy Spirit, as Australia is known in Pentecostal circles. It would be the place from which Pentecostalism would arise and take over the nations of the world, according to the great Pentecostalist Smith Wigglesworth.

Frank Houston's Lower Hutt church decided to bankroll him for two years, so he could set up the first of his Christian Life Centres in Sydney. Later, it would become apparent that some couldn't wait to see the back of him.

———

The Australian Pentecostal scene wasn't quite ready for Frank Houston's revivalist style. The Houstons represented a trend that was too flashy by Australian standards, and at first the Australian Assemblies of God hierarchy resisted them and their theatrics.

The Pentecostal movement had existed on the fringes of Australia's religious landscape for decades. During that time it was largely a phenomenon of country towns and regional Australia. It was big in Queensland, mainly, and then South Australia. This was a time when conservative Pentecostals dared not attend the cinema, lest Jesus return and find them revelling in earthly pleasure. The church executive had issued warnings against 'fleshly dancing, social drinking and rock music'.

The coming of the Houstons heralded a battle for the heart and soul of Australian Pentecostalism. It was a political as well as a spiritual battle, and it all came down to numbers.

Frank had risen to the top of New Zealand's Assemblies of God movement because his style had dragged in a huge number of new followers, along with their money. The same scenario was set to unfold in Australia.

Frank pursued an aggressive growth strategy, which involved teaming up with the biggest names in world Pentecostalism, who travelled to Australia to lend a hand. One was Jimmy Swaggart, the American televangelist and Pentecostal preacher, who was then the hottest property in US evangelism.

Another was the South Korean pastor David Yonggi Cho, who was virtually unknown outside Pentecostal circles, yet his Yoido Full Gospel Church was the largest local Pentecostal church in the world. By the year 2000, it would have membership of more than 700,000.

Yonggi Cho's great trick was to add 'The Gospel of Blessing' to the traditional Pentecostal fourfold gospel: Jesus Saves, Jesus Heals, Jesus Baptises in the Spirit, and Jesus Is Coming Again.

'Blessing' had the overt meaning of 'material blessing'. It was based on an interpretation of the Bible that Christ lived in poverty while on this Earth so that we could live well and be removed from the curse of poverty. (This differs from the more common interpretation that Jesus died to break the curse of sin and death, with this being taken to be the breaking of all curses, and the opening up of all blessings, including money.) If we did not claim our rightful blessings as Children of God, then we were wasting the life of poverty that Christ had led.

This is the central idea of the 'Prosperity Gospel', which Frank Houston quickly embraced. Coupled with the revivalist movement, it propelled the Houstons—both father and son— to radically change Australian Pentecostalism. It dragged a conservative, fringe religion closer to mainstream Australia, and it perfectly aligned Pentecostalism with the values of an aspirational middle class.

Having begun as outsiders, Frank and then Brian Houston moved to the very top of the Assemblies of God movement in Australia.

The takeover left a bitter legacy. Not everyone agreed with the Biblical interpretation that the accumulation of wealth was somehow a reward from God. For one thing, it has the effect of demonising the poor: if you are wealthy because you believe in God, then the flip side is that you are poor because you lack faith.

Those who were vanquished in the battle for the soul of Pentecostalism might ultimately consider that they had right on their side. If it looks dodgy and it sounds dodgy, then maybe it really is dodgy.

The Son

Brian Houston's shining kingdom for Jesus began in the dead-ordinary suburban blocks of north-western Sydney.

Google might have Silicon Valley, but Hillsong had a suburb called Baulkham Hills. It was, and remains, the very picture of consumer Australia: a land of car dealerships, hardware stores and malls bursting at the seams with home furnishing stores, fast-food outlets and coffee nooks for harried mums and dads. And, with all that, an aching emptiness and a yearning for meaning.

Hillsong wasn't always called Hillsong. It was once the Hills Christian Life Centre—a decidedly functional, even dowdy, take on the glamorous pursuit that religion could be. The Hills Christian Life Centre started with a mere dozen people in 'home fellowship' meetings.

From private homes, the meetings moved to a local school hall. As the numbers swelled, Brian and Bobbie Houston moved to yet larger meeting places. A tent was built, then, finally, an auditorium that could accommodate thousands at a time.

With the growth in the Houstons' following and their increased contact with the American megachurch phenomenon came a change in their presentation. Brian went shopping in California and, when he returned, he was suddenly 'funkified', with 'loud shirts', as one who saw all this up close recalled later. Bobbie's dresses were 'suddenly shorter'. They no longer wore typical, conservative Pentecostal clothes. 'It was a total transformation. He left being Brian Houston. And he came back totally different . . . They dressed beautifully and they were attractive. Sexy is the wrong word. But there was sort of like a sanctified sensuality about it.'

In America, Brian had also seen the fruits of 'Prosperity Gospel' preaching. These included the custom of 'love offerings', whereby a church congregation would stump up a cash gift to a visiting pastor, tax-free and often running into many thousands of dollars.

Brian Houston was much changed from the awkward and withdrawn boy of his teenage years. He had morphed into another person altogether. The then 40-year-old senior pastor was now a preacher in the mould of the American televangelists he had met. He had risen to head of the Assemblies of God in Australia, composed of close to a thousand churches, big and small.

Before long, he would be walking among the elite of the evangelical world.

———

For a man of God, Brian Houston had an unorthodox relationship with the powerful and the wealthy: he wanted to be one of them. He also wanted you to be one of them. And unashamedly so. In Houston's world, the devil makes us think small. Houston's god is a god of abundance. Will the meek inherit the earth? Give us a break.

Prosperity sat at the centre of his brand of Pentecostal Christianity, and there was a rationale for it: the more wealth you have, the more influence you have to shape the world. This was the core of the Houston enterprise. Brian Houston might have raised himself up from humble beginnings in New Zealand, and he might have become famous for the church he built in Sydney's suburbs—but these were only steps to the ultimate dream: a world beyond national borders, where Hillsong and Pentecostal Christianity would reign.

There is a network of wealthy American pastors—joined by Brian Houston—which wants to use that power to transform the world, sector by sector. Under the banner of the 'Seven Mountains' mandate, the movement seeks to influence the seven sectors which they consider are vital in shaping society in God's name. The sectors are government, media, arts and entertainment, business, education, religion and family.

The Seven Mountains mandate has a Biblical underpinning—or so Pentecostal Christians say. The relevant verses are Revelation 17:9 ('And here is the mind which hath wisdom. The seven heads are seven mountains') and Isaiah 2:2 ('Now it shall come to pass in the latter days that the mountain of the Lord's house shall be established on the top of the mountains').

Followers believe that, by fulfilling the Seven Mountains mandate, they can bring about the end times, and with it the restoration of God's kingdom.

Houston, very much on board, encouraged his followers to think of themselves as influencers in the world, no matter how small they believed their influence to be.

'They talk about the pillars of society or the spheres of society,' he sermonised in 2017. 'And they include things like government—what a great place for Christians to be. Education. They talk about the arts. Or sport and entertainment. You've got business, commerce. Then you got the media. How much do we need people who love the Lord Jesus Christ, when it comes to the media, and I'm not just talking about people who maybe get to write a little column in the local newspaper.'

Brian Houston had never hidden his intentions. He had been banging on about it ad nauseam for decades. It's just that no one out there in the secular world had been paying attention. Houston wanted influence. He wanted Christians to enforce their world view, their morals and their beliefs. To create systems in which the way of life they saw as being Christ-like became the norm.

The model was the United States, the spiritual home and the financial hub of evangelical Christianity. In dollar terms, it is by far the world's biggest market. Most of all, it is a country where conservative Christian power is genuinely intertwined in the political system and can meaningfully influence the laws governing the life of the nation.

In Australian terms, what says influence more than having a prime minister in the Lodge who looks to you as his mentor? And what beats a personal audience with the President of the United States?

2
ACTS OF THE APOSTLES

Brother Geoff

The transformation of Brian Houston's original 'Hills Christian Life Centre' into 'Hillsong' was inspired by the church's first music pastor, Geoff Bullock. It turned out to be a stroke of genius.

Bullock is a big figure in the history of Hillsong. He goes way back to the early days of the Houstons' reign as Australia's Pentecostal supremos. He made Hillsong famous for its music, and he laid the foundations for the church's extraordinary overseas expansion.

Geoff Bullock's story is its own Hillsong parable. His day job was as a cameraman at the ABC, an experience which leached any idealism from him. He had seen society's leaders close up and become accustomed to the games they played.

'You see a politician before they turn the lights on for an interview, and what they say before and after that red light comes on are completely different things,' he recalls.

Wandering in the desert of his life, Bullock one day happened upon a new kind of church gathering. Following the advice of a friend who was a newly minted Jesus convert, he went along with his girlfriend for a look-see inside Frank Houston's church in inner Sydney, a block or two off the main drag of Oxford Street. It was then a seedy part of town, but Pastor Frank was turning on a performance which captivated Bullock.

'There was just this really interesting buzz. I walked in and Frank preached like something I'd never encountered culturally. It was just so, so different. It wasn't so much a sermon as it was a bit of a show,' he recalls. 'There were lots of exaggerated stories. I'd done lots of things in my life and it was just the oddest night, and eventually my girlfriend and I went down to the front when Frank did the call [for the unchurched to come forward] and we received Jesus as our Lord and Saviour. And that was the whole idea of it. It was just a real worked-up emotion, you know, with the music swelling.'

The Houston magic show was a long way from the standard church fare, with the ageing congregation upstanding for a rendition of 'For Those in Peril on the Sea'. Geoff Bullock had found the answer to the almighty question: *What is the purpose of it all?*

'People would mill around Frank and ask him to lay hands on them and impart the anointing. When you think about it, it's very dangerous because they're not just having a spiritual connection with God. They are having a spiritual connection with the minister, which wasn't questioned. He was seen as a man of God doing God's work, and God was doing his work through this man. It was very unquestioning.

'When Frank first came to Australia, the Assemblies of God hierarchy wouldn't have him. The Christian Life Centre, which he started, really was a church without an accountable structure above them.'

As later events would prove, Bullock's view of the dangers of the preacher's unbridled power was right on the money.

Geoff Bullock had found the elevated, much venerated figure of Frank Houston to be 'aloof'—until he began working with him on music. From then on, his life became more and more entwined with that of the Houstons, and with their ambition for growth.

———

When Brian Houston moved out of his father's shadow to establish his own church, Bullock was right alongside him. Checking out the best areas for potential growth, they settled on Sydney's Hills District.

Bums on seats. Getting the unchurched through the door. Geoff Bullock recalls that it was relentlessly about the numbers.

Those who plant churches have a unique understanding of the rules you have to play by to succeed. After all, the risks are high. Competition for souls is intense. Burnout is common among pastors.

'When we started to build and had got to one hundred and fifty, to two hundred people, we thought, "Wow, that's quite amazing,"' Geoff Bullock recalls. 'They were all young people. Young baby boomers, just married, with little kids, and who'd bought houses out in the north-west.

'We were starting to be invited to play at various functions: Saturday-afternoon church events and such, with churches joining together. And that's when I suggested to Brian that we call the music team Hillsong.'

By the late 1980s, Bullock had tossed in his ABC job and joined Brian Houston as Hillsong's first full-time music pastor.

Bullock ultimately went on to create the music that took Hillsong around the world, attracting more and more souls for Jesus. The genre is soft rock meets soaring vocals, plus inspirational lyrics. Add plenty of repetition and a driving drum beat. All harmonic and no demonic.

As music pastor, Bullock orchestrated weekly performances involving around 40 singers and musicians with a 40-channel mixer, a video projector, three cameras and video screens. He produced several live albums, one of which delivered Hillsong its first platinum record in the United States.

A successful Hillsong composition had energy, power and positivity. It was full of hope and light. In short, it was exactly the kind of music that resonated with the young, aspirational family demographic to which Hillsong played.

It was also the bedrock for the wholesome, family-friendly and, above all, safe environment which the church aimed to create for upwardly mobile communities. The happy family image was embodied in the husband-and-wife team of Brian and Bobbie Houston, perennially dressed in smart casual clothes, looking smooth as silk with big, white-toothed smiles.

What was not to like? Especially when Satan was on the loose in the outside world?

Elder Nabi

There are kingdom builders—and then there's the king of Kingdom Builders.

On the very top rung of the Hillsong enterprise sits a man whose name is virtually unknown to the wider world, but who is the very personification of the church's prosperity gospel. For a period of 30 years dating back to the 1990s, he has been key to protecting the church's reputation.

Hillsong has a handful of Kingdom Builders—a special class of mega donors whose donations are measured in the tens of thousands of dollars. They include the Denton brothers, Phillip and Andrew (no relation to the media personality), who own the Hillscorp property development company, which operates mainly in south-east Queensland. None, though, has been more influential than Nabi Saleh, who has been on board with the Houstons since the 1980s.

The fabulously wealthy Saleh has been one of Hillsong's whale donors. He has sat at the right hand of Brian Houston. He has been a key link man to the multimillionaire American preachers in Houston's orbit. Saleh is also a canny business operator. The businessman, originally from Iran, also represents one of the great prizes in the world of Christian evangelism: a convert to Christianity from Islam.

Brian Houston has never been able to praise him highly enough. Saleh 'has been one of my closest, dearest friends for more than thirty years', Houston declared in one Hillsong sermon. 'He was a Shiite Muslim. And he got radically saved. And today he's a tremendous, tremendous believer and example in our church, being one of the most loyal and committed and releasing people to Bobbie and I, over thirty years.'

There is no convert as sweet as one drawn from a competing religion. In Saleh's case, Brian Houston had the fire-breathing American preacher Kenneth Copeland to thank: Saleh converted after hearing the charismatic evangelical fabulist at a convention in 1979.

Houston's praise of Nabi Saleh came during a sermon on the topic of money and how to use your influence to change society's institutions. Nabi, as Houston recalled, was 'well off' even when he arrived at the church.

'I remember looking at Nabi: generous, a giver, and just his whole releasing spirit. And I pray to God there can be more like Nabi. And I'll just be honest with you. I think I was thinking: "Now, Lord, bring more millionaires through the door. But not just millionaires, but people who've got that big spirit—people who are huge on the inside, who just see possibility and want to see you fulfil that possibility."'

———

Nabi Saleh does not seek fame. He is so low profile in the church that even other churchgoers might not recognise him, but his business interests have had global prominence. Saleh made his fortune out of coffee, in particular the international Gloria Jean's operation, which his family once co-owned.

Saleh landed in the Hills District and entered Brian Houston's world via an unorthodox route. He was born in Shiraz, Iran. His corporate records also say he has a degree in science, and that he came to Australia via India in 1973 at the age of 24. But Saleh's first port of call had been to work in the coffee plantations of Papua New Guinea, where he established his name as a supplier.

Gloria Jean's Coffees was the perfect example of the symbiotic relationship between business and church. Nabi Saleh's partner in Gloria Jean's was another wealthy Hillsong figure, Peter Irvine, who had built a career in advertising. Together, Saleh and Irvine bought the Australian franchising rights in 1995 and were so successful that, over time, they ended up acquiring the US owner of the Gloria Jean's brand and most of the international branding, roasting and franchising rights. At the same time, Saleh was on the board of Hillsong and already an indispensable member of the Houston team and an adviser to both Frank and Brian.

Those attending Hillsong could buy a Gloria Jean's coffee from a stall in the foyer. A number of Gloria Jean's franchises were owned by Hillsong members, who then gave a 10 per cent tithe of their pre-tax income to the church. Other Pentecostal churches, too, had a Gloria Jean's cafe in their building. It was commonly known and appreciated in Christian circles that they were Christian coffee shops.

At various times, Gloria Jean's was the cause of troublesome publicity for Hillsong, briefly exposing some senior members of the church to the glare of bad press.

Media reports in 2008 revealed that Gloria Jean's cafes around Australia supported the activities of a Hillsong-linked rehab facility for women called Mercy Ministries. Mercy Ministries claimed to provide professional residential counselling support for young women needing help with eating disorders, depression, self-harm, unplanned pregnancies, drug and alcohol abuse, and the effects of sexual or physical abuse.

But their 'counselling program' consisted of prayer, Christian counselling and exorcisms to expel 'demons' from the young women, many of whom had serious psychiatric conditions. The facility was eventually shut down and its directors were forced to issue a public apology.

Mercy Ministries' directors included Peter Irvine, Gloria Jean's co-owner, among other high-profile Hillsong figures. Gloria Jean's cafes carried promotional material and a donation box for the rehab facility.

Gloria Jean's was also revealed to have paid $30,000 to the Australian Christian Lobby (ACL). Following a customer backlash, the coffee chain defended the payment as being for commercial reasons, and 'not an endorsement' of the 'views and values' of the ACL, which included fierce opposition to homosexuality and same-sex marriage. Investigations also showed that Gloria Jean's holding company, Jireh International Pty Ltd, had donated funds which arrived via a third party to the conservative Family First political party.

Nabi Saleh and Peter Irvine ultimately sold the worldwide rights to the Gloria Jean's franchise in 2014 for close to $200 million. Earlier that year, a Gloria Jean's franchise in Melbourne was fined $110,000 for underpaying staff following an investigation by the Fair Work Ombudsman, which found that 22 workers were paid as little as $8 per hour (around half the minimum wage).

What is hard to measure is the impact of the commercial nous which the businessman brought to Hillsong as it built its international network of corporate entities.

The many spokes of Hillsong have ended up all linking back to Hillsong's US operation. Its worldwide activities look and smell just like a franchise model, this one for Pentecostal Christianity.

The parallels are compelling. Saleh started out as co-owner of the Gloria Jean's coffee franchise for Australia. He later worked a form of reverse takeover, by which he and Irvine acquired the US company, which owned the global franchising business.

Hillsong began as an outpost of a US-style evangelical operation. It later moved to America, the world headquarters of prosperity evangelism. Like Gloria Jean's, Hillsong-linked churches around the world have access to Hillsong branding, Hillsong music and—no doubt—Hillsong's pastors, who will breeze through for a paid speaking gig.

The franchise model also guarantees a steady percentage flow of funds to corporate HQ—at the rate of up to 5 per cent of parishioners' tithes and donations, depending on how close the relationship is to the Hillsong mothership.

Alongside his lucrative commercial dealings, Saleh found time to cultivate relationships with several of the United States' leading evangelical preachers. He became the director of an Australian-registered charity, Shiloh Ministries Australia, along with two of Brian Houston's favourite American preachers,

Casey Treat and Rick Godwin. Brian Houston has nominated the two—who also became authors and motivational speakers—as being among the most influential in his life.

Saleh has for several years been closely linked with a prominent Texas-based pastor, Dr Jerry Savelle, as a director of the Australian offshoot of Jerry Savelle Ministries International. Jerry Savelle broadcasts his message in 200 countries worldwide; his Australian organisation operates from the Gold Coast and is registered with the Australian Charities and Not-for-profits Commission (ACNC).

Saleh has also been a long-term director of another organisation registered as an Australian charity, and which bears a rather cumbersome name: Kenneth Copeland Ministries Eagle Mountain International Church Ltd. This is the local vehicle for the multimillionaire US pastor Kenneth Copeland. In the small world of elite Pentecostalism, Jerry Savelle and Kenneth Copeland work closely together; Savelle has also been a director of Kenneth Copeland Ministries in the United States.

As a key link between these hugely popular pastors and Houston's Hillsong operation, Nabi Saleh has positioned himself as arguably the most powerful and most influential Pentecostal figure in Australia, even though Brian Houston has always been the one in the limelight.

In the story of the 'Till on the Hill', as the Hillsong money machine is derisively known, Nabi Saleh has been both financial wizard and trusted advisor to the main man.

No wonder Brian Houston prayed to God for more Nabis.

Mind you, there was a Scott in the wings who would also have a big part to play in driving the fortunes of Hillsong and Pentecostalism in Australia.

Brother Scott

Just when the Houstons were building Hillsong into a national force, from out of left field a young university student was showing an unusually intense level of interest in the art of stimulating church growth. The student's name was Scott Morrison, and he was studying economic geography at the University of New South Wales.

The young Morrison had been a denomination switcher himself. Beginning in the Uniting Church, he then spent time at the Baptist Church as well as with the Open Brethren Assemblies (sometimes called the Christian Brethren), a socially conservative church with roots stemming back to England's Plymouth Brethren. The closed version of the Brethren Church, the Exclusive Brethren, forbids women from work outside the family and it has its own education system.

Later, as Australia's first Pentecostal prime minister, Morrison spoke of his lifelong preference for 'community churches', such as the Baptist, Brethren and Assemblies of God Pentecostal churches. While an occasional visitor to Hillsong events, Morrison ultimately chose to attend a Pentecostal church in his southern Sydney electorate. The church had been established by a former Hillsong pastor.

'That's where I want to be, in a church that believes in community and creates community,' he told a conference of

Australia's Pentecostal church leaders. 'And the essence of community is each individual understanding that they're valued, that they're unique. That they can respect one another. That they can contribute to one another.'

At age 21, Morrison researched and wrote a 150-page thesis on Sydney's Brethren churches, and strategies to make them bigger and increase their influence. It was an unusual choice for a future prime minister. Most of Morrison's immediate predecessors as PM—Malcolm Turnbull, Tony Abbott, Julia Gillard and John Howard—had all qualified in law. Kevin Rudd had a first-class honours degree in Chinese studies.

Today, Morrison's thesis—submitted as part of his UNSW honours degree—can be found in a specialist Brethren collection at the University of Manchester. It is described there as a 'micro approach' to the relationship between religion and society, using a study of the Christian Brethren Assemblies of Sydney as the focus.

Morrison found that Sydney's Brethren Assemblies were in a period of transition. Close examination revealed that the movement had experienced 'a net loss to other denominations'. His demographic analysis showed that the Brethren Assemblies had 'failed to relate' to large sections of the metropolitan community, particularly 'those employed in blue-collar occupations, the unemployed, those without tertiary qualifications and those born overseas'. It is easy to see here the mind of a political campaign strategist at work, matching his product to demographic needs and desires.

Morrison's view was that the Assemblies should 'maintain the standard and emphasis placed upon Bible teaching', but that they 'must realise' that this alone 'will not bring about growth'. 'Visitation' and 'counselling' were also important.

The honours student warned that, unless the churches embraced change, the impression of them as 'a white-collar institution' would only be further entrenched. Morrison's prescription was to go for growth by having the church engage in more 'bridge-building' activities with the community. Marketing. Always marketing.

Morrison, as a young evangelist, commended the work of influential American Christian Jim Petersen, and in particular his book *Evangelism for Our Generation*, which documented a style of evangelism that was receiving 'an increasing amount of attention around the world today'.

Petersen, having spent decades working with those he called 'the unchurched', was passing on the secrets of how to develop relationships with 'the unreached', how to model the Christian message and how to present the Bible's claims 'in a non-threatening manner'.

Petersen's approach included 'church planting', which was already being done in Sydney's western suburbs and in the suburbs surrounding Brisbane by Assembly workers. Critically, though, it also involved church members taking up an active role in the community in activities such as 'P&C associations, Neighbourhood Watch, sporting clubs, local interest groups and other such community-based organisations and activities', Morrison wrote.

'The idea of this approach is to restore the interpersonal component to evangelism,' he concluded. 'It has been described as "bringing the church to the people" whereas past approaches have involved bringing people to the church. It attempts to personalise what has often been seen by the community as an abstract or irrelevant institution.' This would lead to 'church growth, particularly through conversion'.

Scott Morrison's work was niche, but its 'bringing it to the people' strategy applied absolutely to the growth of the Assemblies of God (or Pentecostal) churches. It is not clear whether the committed young Christian had any interest in politics while at university. It was a decade later that he emerged from the New South Wales Liberal Party.

But what is clear is that, by the time he left university, Morrison was a fluent speaker of 'Christianese'. This is a language of its own and consists of words like 'planting' and 'unchurched', as well as phrases snatched from the Bible, such as 'blessed to be a blessing'. Such words and their nuances of meaning are known to insiders, while remaining a mystery to everybody else.

———

One of Scott Morrison's oft-repeated stories involves the birth of his and Jenny's first daughter, Abbey, after more than a decade of failed attempts through IVF.

Abbey was born on 7 July 2007: the seventh of the seventh of the seventh. Morrison has described this coming-together of sevens as being no accident and a constant reminder of 'who's in charge'.

Speaking to a Pentecostal gathering shortly after he had lost his prime ministership, he added a new twist to the story. His wife, Jenny, had been well and truly ready to give birth on the morning of 6 July 2007. And yet the day wore on . . . and on . . . but the birth did not occur.

'And as we got to later that night, it started to twig to me what was going on,' he said. 'And Abbey was born soon after, at one am on the seventh of the seventh of the seventh. And you know, what that said to me was that God is faithful.'

To the assembled Pentecostal believers, the confluence of sevens was proof that former Prime Minister Morrison was not just anyone: he was very special indeed in the eyes of God.

The night he won the 2019 election, a beaming Morrison had declared loudly and purposefully that he had *always* believed in miracles—a nod to the Acts of the Apostles and the Feast of Pentecost. It was a signal to believers that God had chosen one of their own for this time in history, to restore the conditions of the day of Pentecost.

3
NUMBERS

The American Template

When it comes to cashing in on faith, America's preachers are hard to beat, but Brian Houston has given them a run for their money.

Pentecostal televangelist Jim Bakker and his 'Praise the Lord' ministries raked in millions upon millions of dollars before collapsing in the late 1980s. The excesses of the preacher man and his wife, Tammy Faye, were extraordinary. The Bakkers had been paid about US$1.6 million in bonuses and salaries a year in the mid-1980s. Their possessions included a 16-metre houseboat, a $45,000 Mercedes-Benz, a $55,000 Rolls-Royce, and homes and apartments in South Carolina, Tennessee and Florida.

Pentecostal preacher Jimmy Swaggart, who had built a massive national and international following via his *Camp Meeting Hour* television show, came unstuck around the same time. Swaggart had previously teamed up with Frank Houston to help put some wind under the wings of the Assemblies of God movement in Australia.

There were others, too, who had a long-lasting impact. Robert Schuller and his mighty Crystal Cathedral rose out of California, built with the money of his worldwide followers. The Reverend Jerry Falwell, co-founder of the Moral Majority, and Pat Robertson both built financial fortunes and immense political influence in America's conservative politics.

Brian Houston followed the example of these prosperity gospel preachers who had flourished in the America of the 1980s and 1990s; he became close friends with many of them. The success of the US evangelical churches held lessons for Hillsong.

America's evangelical Christian movement had grafted itself onto the small-government ethos—or, better still, the no-government ethos—of neoliberal economics. The bigger you are, the more political influence you have; and the more political influence you have, the less government will get in your way and the bigger you can become. It's a virtuous circle of growth begetting power without the state interfering. Somewhat para-doxically, you can even use your power to insist that the state gives you special support.

On one level, it is market economics at work. On another level, for some, it is God's will. Even better, maybe, for a believer, it is the two combined.

———

Among the leading lights of American evangelism are Kenneth and Gloria Copeland. They make a fine couple. Kenneth still has his dark, wavy hair, even in his late eighties. Gloria stands wrinkle-free and straight-backed next to her pastor husband, with a string of pearls draped around her neck and the bobbed blonde hair of a woman one-third her age.

The Copelands seem perennially to smile with the serenity of the godly. Yet Kenneth can launch into a righteous, table-thumping fury to denounce the devil in God's name. Kenneth has also made a confession about what he does in bed before he goes to sleep, a little secret he passed on via his ministry website:

> The last thing that comes out of my mouth, so quiet that Gloria is not able to hear me, is this: 'I love the Lord my God with all my heart, with all my soul, with all my mind and with all my strength. I love my neighbour as myself, and I love the brethren even as You love the brethren. Thank You, Lord Jesus, for loving me. Thank You for loving my family and for taking care of us as You have all these years. I love You so. I love You so.'

It's easy to see why the Copelands are happy with their lot. 'Brother Kenneth', also known as 'The Prophet' by his church, is estimated to be worth over a billion dollars, the result of a 50-year career preaching the prosperity gospel. His example has made him a potent force in America's conservative politics, where he was part of Donald Trump's Evangelical Executive Advisory Board. He stood side by side with Trump during the 2022 midterm elections, urging evangelical Christians to support the 'Make America Great Again' movement.

In a way, given how fabulously wealthy and powerful Kenneth Copeland is, you'd have to be nuts not to follow in his footsteps. And that's precisely what the Houstons have done. Hillsong and Brian Houston have various touchpoints with Kenneth Copeland Ministries.

Brian and Bobbie paid fawning public tribute to Kenneth on the 40-year commemoration of Kenneth Copeland Ministries, which has a branch in Australia.

'Well, Kenneth Copeland, and your beautiful wife, Gloria,' Houston began, 'we want to thank you for forty great years of ministry in our great country, Australia, teaching, preaching, pointing people to Jesus, encouraging people to live by faith and to see kingdom possibilities. We are very proud to know you and very, very blessed by the work that you have done. And thank God for the impact that you have had on people like us and on churches like Hillsong. And I want to just encourage you to keep on going, There's more to come.'

As Brian spoke, Bobbie nodded appreciatively alongside.

Hillsong elder Nabi Saleh, as we have seen, was converted to Christianity by Copeland and has fronted for him in Australia for more than 25 years, as a director of Kenneth Copeland Ministries Eagle Mountain International Church Ltd. As mentioned earlier the organisation is registered as a charity, and enjoys a range of tax breaks, notwithstanding the extreme wealth of the Copeland organisation.

Copeland's approach has made him a figure both revered and reviled in the United States. In later years he has drawn scorn for the bizarre nature of his church performances. These have included commanding Covid-19 to disappear, as though he were Moses parting the Red Sea with his staff. With a demonic glint in his eye, and puffing out his cheeks with the 'Breath of God', he claims to be able to literally blow away the virus. In 2020, he claimed that the pandemic had ended or would soon end, and that his followers would be healed from the virus. He stated that followers should continue paying tithes if they lost their jobs in the economic crisis that the pandemic caused. He has also ceremonially mixed his own blood with what he called 'the Blood of Christ' and supped on the concoction in front of his congregation.

Copeland makes no efforts to hide his wealth. Indeed, it is his selling point. He rarely gives interviews to the secular media, but in 2019 a reporter from the US current-affairs program *Inside Edition* managed to corral him. With no shame he justified his lavish lifestyle. Perhaps surprisingly for a man of God, this includes a small fleet of private jets and holiday homes dotted around the country.

When asked how he responded to those who say preachers shouldn't live so luxuriously, Copeland said simply: 'They're wrong. It's a misunderstanding of the Bible . . . Abraham was a very, very wealthy man,' he explained. 'Galatians, chapter 3: "If you belong to Christ, then are you Abraham's seed and heirs according to His promise." And his promise was great wealth.'

The reporter objected: 'The Bible also said that it's more difficult for a rich man to get into heaven than it is for a camel to pass through the eye of a needle.'

'Ah,' Copeland butted in, adding the rest of the scripture, 'he said *all* things are possible with God.'

How do you argue with that?

———

The American televangelists work by a well-worn template that aims to maximise income while minimising accountability. The template also puts a premium on continuous growth and expansion. Their 'ministries' are typically constructed as multi-faceted businesses that sell books, videos and music on top of their core work of preaching to congregations, online and in person.

There are normally dedicated ministries for children, teen-agers and women. The larger organisations have their own studios for recording and broadcasting music. Some have established their own universities or Bible colleges. They have 'outreach' services for the poor and rehab facilities for those experiencing addiction or trauma. They fund overseas aid projects.

Some pastors are prolific publishers of books. Jerry Savelle—a close associate of Kenneth Copeland and of Hillsong's Nabi Saleh—has published more than 70 titles. Joyce Meyer, the best-known female preacher in the United States, has written double that number. Meyer's books are in the self-help genre, with snappy titles like *20 Ways to Make Every Day Better*. Many pastors produce and market music under their own religious labels.

The churches are highly corporatised, with a maze of corporate entities registered in different jurisdictions. Many have been run by boards composed of the senior pastor's family and trusted friends. The senior pastor has near total power.

Most of the 'churches' are non-denominational—not so as to create a broader 'Christian' church, but rather to avoid the accountability that comes with being a member of a denomination, such as the Methodist Church, that has regulatory powers.

The churches have also sought to bring as much of their work as possible into the structure of a not-for-profit organisation or charity, thereby ensuring they pay little or no tax while also taking advantage of secrecy provisions. Because of this secrecy, it is hard to know to what extent the church funds the senior pastor's lifestyle.

Several church staff might be 'ordained' as ministers to take advantage of tax-free housing.

Over the years, Hillsong adopted nearly all these features.

A Vision of Wealth

Kenneth Copeland has been unwilling to reveal the detail of his wealth and, in particular, to separate his personal wealth from that of his church. Most of what is publicly known about him and his modus operandi comes from a US Senate probe into the affairs of six American televangelists, which reported in 2011. The investigation was initiated by Senator Chuck Grassley, a Republican who had opened an inquiry into the tax-exempt religious sector; the work of his committee brought to the attention of Americans (and the rest of the world) the ostentatious lifestyles of the prosperity gospel preachers.

'The tax-exempt sector is so big that, from time to time, certain practices draw public concern,' Grassley said at the time. 'My goal is to help improve accountability and good governance so tax-exempt groups maintain public confidence in their operations.'

The inquiry into Kenneth Copeland Ministries revealed that Copeland owned a private airport, and that he—or his organisation—owned two jets, a Gulfstream V and a Cessna Citation X (the latter bought for US$20 million), as well as smaller aircraft.

Kenneth and Gloria had the run of a luxurious three-storey mansion of 1.7 square kilometres fronting a lake near Fort Worth, Texas. This was the church 'parsonage'.

The Senate review found that the humble Copeland home included some finishing touches to die for. There was the sweeping spiral staircase, as well as an enclosed air bridge connecting the two wings of the outsized mansion. There were crystal chandeliers and feature doors, which, according to Gloria, came originally from a castle in Europe. The Copeland bedroom had a huge drop-down ceiling projector and screen. There were garages at either end of the house, where the Copelands kept their motorcycles, luxury cars and a golf cart.

It emerged that employees of the Copeland organisation maintained the property and performed 'miscellaneous duties', such as arranging the Copelands' exercise equipment, moving their furniture and setting up their Christmas tree.

Was it extravagant? Copeland later claimed that God had told him years earlier to build this dream home, which Gloria had described to him. Her vision had included a three-storey mansion with long white columns at the front.

'Minister this house to her,' he recalled being told. 'It is part of your prosperity.'

Apart from the Copelands' sheer wealth, the Grassley probe shone a light on the 'honorarium' racket, where pastors of one church are paid large tax-free sums to speak at events held by other churches. Kenneth and Gloria Copeland had both received such honorariums, normally at the rate of US$10,000 per appearance.

Most instructive, though, was the corporate structure of Kenneth Copeland Ministries. Members of the governing board were family or close associates of the Copelands. And under the constitutions of the many different organisations under the Copeland umbrella, Pastor Kenneth had the power of veto over all decisions.

The tentacles of the Copeland Ministries business model spread into music and inspirational books written by Kenneth and Gloria, yielding the couple more bundles of cash in royalties. Kenneth Copeland Ministries was registered under 'at least 21 assumed names' with the state of Texas. These included record companies and recording studios.

'This raises the question of whether church status is being gamed to shield such activities of a tax-exempt entity from public scrutiny,' the Grassley review noted, while questioning whether the US Congress ever intended for a multimillion-dollar enterprise such as the Copeland Ministries to be exempt from filing a full declaration of its assets to the Internal Revenue Service.

That question went to the heart of what it means to be a religious charity, and the attendant exemptions from paying tax an organisation might receive if it is, in fact, a business. That same issue would rear its head in Australia.

Ultimately, the Senate failed to complete its inquiries satisfactorily because four of the six televangelists simply refused to cooperate. The Copeland organisation went out of its way to prevent the Grassley committee from gaining any information. In an indicator of the kind of hardball that the prosperity churches can play, not only did it refuse to cooperate with the committee's requests, but it also used what committee staff termed 'strong tactics' to prevent former employees from speaking.

'Several former employees' indicated that the Copeland organisation had used intimidation in an attempt to keep them from speaking to the committee, staff investigators reported. 'Former employees were sincerely afraid to provide statements for fear of being sued since they signed confidentiality agreements. Employees were contacted by [Copeland organisation] attorneys ... and reminded that they signed a confidentiality agreement agreeing not to disclose any information concerning the organisation.'

One former employee told the Senate committee:

The Copelands employ guerrilla tactics to keep their employees silent. We are flat out told and threatened that if we talk, God will blight our finances, strike our families down, and pretty much afflict us with everything evil and unholy. Rather, God will allow Satan to do those things to us because we have stepped out from under His umbrella of protection, by 'touching God's anointed Prophet'. Further, employees are encouraged to shun and treat badly anyone who dares speak out.

Kenneth Copeland is a leading proponent of the idea—also advocated by Brian Houston—that Christians should 'reign' in the seven spheres of influence that dominate society.

Using the language typical of the evangelical vision of world domination, Copeland tells his followers that praying for 'Godly leaders' to rise up within each cultural sphere matters, because 'you are attacking the enemy's plan in that particular realm and taking back the dominion that rightfully belongs to us, as Christians'.

Houston and Copeland share a spiritual lineage back to the late American preacher Oral Roberts. Copeland waxes dewy-eyed of his time as Roberts' personal pilot, when he flew the charismatic Christian televangelist around the country, laying the foundations of the prosperity gospel. He laments that, just like Roberts, he is taking 'the same heat for believing God would prosper you'.

Roberts influenced Australian Pentecostalism through the tent tours the Oral Roberts Evangelistic Association conducted in Australia in the 1950s. Brian Houston held a seat for a number of years on the board of reference attached to Oral Roberts University in Tulsa, Oklahoma.

Brian Houston and Hillsong have also enjoyed close relations with another of the six televangelists on the Grassley hit list. Joyce Meyer Ministries is a different kettle of fish from Copeland. But the only female preacher in the top echelon of American evangelical preachers has made excruciatingly large amounts of money from the business of the prosperity gospel.

In the male-dominated world of evangelical preaching, Meyer's pitch to women is distinctive, powerful and lucrative. She is straight-talking and no-frills—a voice right out of lower-middle-class Missouri. Her sermons are peppered with 'you know what I'm talking about, ladies' anecdotes, usually delivered with a wink and a rueful laugh.

The issue which defines Meyer above all else is her personal story of surviving abuse. It is a pin-drop moment in her sermons when she reveals that she was the subject of constant sexual abuse by her father. Her message is that faith in the Lord overcomes all. You gain strength by forgiving your attacker. Taken to its logical conclusion, the message from Joyce Meyer to victims is to heal through your religion, rather than through the secular world of police courts, convictions and compensation. Meyer's self-help guides have sold millions of copies around the world. Indeed, they have been indispensable to generations of Christian girls and women.

Joyce Meyer Ministries has operated in Australia for around the same time as Kenneth Copeland Ministries, and from the same Brisbane suburb. Meyer herself has taken ministry with Bobbie Houston and delivered her message of forgiveness to Hillsong's annual conference in Sydney. Her ministry's 'Hand of Hope' offshoot partnered with Hillsong for fieldwork in response to Australia's 2019 bushfires.

Meyer has been the subject of a major newspaper investigation in the United States, which revealed her own level of excess—Kenneth Copeland Lite, if you will. The *St. Louis Post-Dispatch* reported that she too had a corporate jet, and her husband drove a US$107,000 silver-grey Mercedes-Benz. 'Meyer is fond of nice things and is willing to spend for them,' the newspaper concluded. From an $11,000 French clock in the ministry's headquarters to a $105,000 Crownline boat docked behind her vacation home at Lake of the Ozarks, it's clear her tastes run more to Perrier than to tap water.

> The ministry's headquarters is a three-storey jewel of red brick and emerald-colour glass that, from the outside, has the look and feel of a luxury resort hotel. Built two years ago for $20 million, the building and grounds are postcard perfect, from manicured flower beds and walkways to a five-storey lighted cross.

Meyer's straight-talking response to these revelations was: 'You can be a businessman here in St. Louis, and people think the more you have, the more wonderful it is. But if you're a preacher, then all of a sudden it becomes a problem. The Bible says, "Give and it shall be given unto you."'

But the newspaper's investigations forced Joyce Meyer Ministries to change its ways. The organisation pledged to voluntarily submit to an annual audit by an independent public accounting firm, in addition to an annual legal audit. It would also reveal the payments made to Joyce Meyer and would require board members and employees to abide by a conflict-of-interest policy that encouraged 'high standards of ethics and integrity'.

Joyce Meyer Ministries declared to the Grassley inquiry that a majority of its board directors were individuals with 'no familial connection with the Meyers', and were not employed 'in any manner' by Joyce Meyer Ministries.

Hillsong, unfortunately, has failed to match many of these standards.

——

Another American preacher in Brian Houston's extensive network is Rick Godwin, a Texas-based pastor who has been a close friend since the 1990s, when Hillsong was in lift-off mode.

Godwin, too, has been forced to answer allegations of extravagant spending in his use of church money. In a filing to a Texas court, a former member of Godwin's Eagle's Nest Christian Fellowship Church deposed that, according to church sources, Godwin was spending hundreds of thousands of dollars of church funds on Armani suits, Cartier watches and chartered jets for personal travel by himself, his family and friends, including members of the church's board of elders. The former member alleged that church employees were aware of the ongoing financial improprieties, but feared losing their jobs if they exposed the wrongdoing.

After these newspaper reports, Godwin reportedly told the congregation he had paid back all personal expenses and launched a new tax compliance audit, among other corrective measures. The case ended after the church argued successfully that the civil courts had no jurisdiction to examine the inner workings of the church.

Rick Godwin is on the board of a charity registered in Australia alongside Nabi Saleh. The two are directors of Shiloh Ministries Australia, alongside yet another US pastor and close Houston friend, Casey Treat.

Why would two United States–domiciled prosperity gospel preachers be part of an Australian charity? Shiloh is categorised as a small charity, despite the evident wealth of its directors, and as such it is not required to disclose its finances. It does, however, receive Australian tax exemptions, just like Kenneth Copeland's outfit.

It Takes Money to Build a Kingdom

Brian Houston has never been shy about being an evangelist for wealth. As Hillsong set down its roots in Sydney's Hills District, he published his manifesto on the power of money, called *You Need More Money*.

In one sense, he was simply following the lead of the American preachers, adding book publishing to the growing business empire and branding of Hillsong Inc. But his 1999 book is so effusive in its praise of money that it is a bracing read. It is as though the Hollywood apostle of corporate greed, Gordon Gekko, has been enlisted as co-author. Certainly the 'greed is good' ethos echoes throughout its pages.

Houston summons up a verse from the Bible as justification for the provocative title. Ecclesiastes 10:19 tells us: 'A feast is made for laughter, and wine makes merry, but money answers everything.' Houston put the final three words in bold and then repeated them in capitals: 'That is what it says: MONEY ANSWERS EVERYTHING.' Just in case you missed it.

What follows is a series of arguments on the benefits of money. It is the answer to hunger. It is the short-term solution to poverty. It answers the 'powerlessness' you might feel in your life, because it enables you to be 'influential'. Written in the style of a self-help manual, the book suggests that '[i]t's time to relax and become more comfortable around money':

> It may involve a little exercise, like putting on your best clothes and ordering coffee in a fancy restaurant or a hotel lobby. Even though you could make the coffee for half the price at home, the total experience may enlarge your thinking. You may even feel better about yourself and life.
>
> I challenge you to do something that will *break* any poverty thinking and guilt that has a hold on you. It may only take one cup of coffee, but it's a step in the right direction of making you feel more comfortable about money.

Many years later, Houston, in an interview with Christian radio station Hope 103.2, nominated writing *You Need More Money* as the one regret of his life:

> It was a great idea to have a controversial title to a book. No-one knew who I was, really and so I didn't have too much influence.

But of course, it became like a bullseye on my forehead, in terms of getting attacked. And a lot of what I wrote in the book, I still would stand by as it was really about being a blessing. It wasn't about getting rich and piling up money, it was about being in a position to be a blessing . . . but it was poorly written, and it was too easy to take it out of context.

'Being a blessing', in Houston's terms, means having the financial ability to help others. But what does *that* mean?

A constant theme in Houston's preaching is that influence equals power, and that power resides in the famous Seven Mountains of influence: government, media, arts and entertainment, business, education, religion and family.

The other side of the coin is that to live a life that is not full of wealth is to succumb to Satan and 'to allow the devil to keep [people] small, to keep them bound up by what they cannot do, and what they can afford', as Houston himself has sermonised.

So accumulating wealth is one in the eye for Satan, as well as funding the work of saving souls for Jesus.

———

The Hillsong business model is simple: it is about getting as much income as possible, while spending as little as possible on things that the church deems to be extraneous. The latter include paying taxation to the state, payments to workers and financial compensation to victims of abuse. It is a model built on the concept that Hillsong exists separate to, and independent of, the state. (Except when it comes to government grants and tax breaks, of course.)

The cornerstone of Hillsong's income is tithing, a pledge of 10 per cent of your pre-tax income as a church follower. The church receives this tax-free, and it accounts for tens of millions of dollars in income every year.

The practice is controversial. It feels archaic, and for those on low incomes it can be a crushing imposition—not to mention those living on government benefits, although they are not Hillsong's target demographic.

Brian Houston has defended tithing on the grounds that it is an obligation to give to God that has its origin in the Bible. 'I've heard many arguments on why one should or shouldn't tithe,' he wrote in *You Need More Money*. 'It is sad that there is so much confusion and debate about a simple task of giving ten per cent of your income to God. Tithing is an eternal principle, I believe, like sowing and reaping.'

Houston acknowledges that the Old Testament's references to tithing were 'done away with in the New Testament'. However, he has an answer to that: he believes that tithing was firmly established and understood in Jewish society at the time of Jesus and the early church.

Hillsong has clubs for those it calls 'Kingdom Builders' and 'Vision Impacters'. They are the members who donate large sums of money to the church, on top of their tithes. You can also make a donation to the annual 'Heart for the House' appeal, which goes to fund Hillsong's chosen charitable works.

Collecting this money has been, for Hillsong, as easy as falling off a log. The church provides as many ways to pay as you want. It's evolved over the years from cash to credit card (in person or online), to electronic funds transfer from your bank account, and then to using the Hillsong app.

If you're in any doubt about tithing, the website gives you another Biblical verse to back it up:

In Malachi, the Bible talks about bringing the first 10% (tithe) of our income into the storehouse (church). If you do, 'I will open the windows of heaven for you. I will pour out a blessing so great you won't have enough room to take it in!' Let's believe for God to provide for us as a church, as we obey His Word in bringing our tithes.

The giving of money is so embedded in the Hillsong way that it becomes completely unexceptional. A former long-term member of the church recalls how surprised she was to discover the low priority put on money at a traditional church.

'When I moved on from Hillsong I went to an Anglican Church near my house,' she says. 'And I just thought it was so weird that they didn't take up an offering, and almost ungodly. All they had was a little lockbox on the back door that you could put money into if you wanted. And I just thought, "This isn't good. Like, people should be generous, and there should be no shame in talking about it." And I think that just probably shows you how much I had to unlearn from my years in Hillsong.'

The organisation has also brought in tens of millions of dollars through its commercial operations, mainly in licensing its music to other churches or through album sales. None of the income from its businesses is taxed, courtesy of federal Australian laws which say that religious charities are entitled to tax breaks if the money they generate through their businesses is channelled into advancing religion.

And what's in it for those parishioners who have given over all that money?

The church regularly publishes success stories of how a person's faith in God has been repaid. Its Facebook posts are full of stories of God's blessings. Like testimonials for washing powder, Hillsong donors attest to how their lives have been changed.

'We have seen extraordinary things achieved through Kingdom Builders and our own finances transformed,' say 'Simon and Kristina'.

'I realised that it is possible to use money for eternal purposes! That God gives us the ability to take something temporary, like money, and turn it into something eternal—I still can't fully comprehend what an incredible exchange is available to us!' says Louisa.

'Looking back over the years we have been attending and volunteering at Hillsong, we have always felt encouraged, empowered and equipped to grow personally and especially when it comes to our business,' say 'Sam and Joanna'.

There's the husband who was desperately in need of a job; he not only gained a part-time job at a restaurant, but was soon promoted to the position of manager.

One grateful Kingdom Builder donor wrote of how their faith in God helped turn around their ailing business, to the point that they were able to secure 'several government contracts', make a profit and expand their 'opportunities'.

One couple was blessed with a child after giving up hope on IVF treatment.

A regular attendee saw his real estate portfolio expand to seven houses with God's blessing.

Many of these testimonials echo the stories of miracles told in Pentecostal lore, when faith healers had the blind seeing again and the crippled walking.

For Kingdom Builder donors, there has been the opportunity of four breakfasts a year and going away on a retreat with Brian Houston—and much more, if you were prepared to up your giving. Said one Kingdom Builder:

I just wanted to double what I gave every year. So the next year $10,000, the next year $20,000, the next year, $40,000 and so on. And they were always my business goals because there was no point in having that money for me.

On those Kingdom Builder retreats it was all focused on making money, sometimes sessions with external people speaking on money and wealth, because we just completely believed that if you have wealth it's just a gift that you have on your life that you could share.

But we were treated very specially in that group. You know, we went away to our little retreats to the

Hunter Valley, where there was an abundance of seafood and great accommodation.

Setting up a special networking group for the wealthy might run directly counter to the ideals of Christianity but it is an essential feature of the Hillsong prosperity model.

One leading Kingdom Builder, businessman Andrew Denton, even wrote a book, published in 2020, in praise of the Kingdom Builder concept.

Denton, who describes himself as an 'Aussie plumber in clean clothes' in a nod to his humble beginnings, had made the decision to go 'all in' with God. He then came to know his purpose in life. It was 'to finance the Kingdom'. He was writing his book because he believed that God was raising up 'an army' of Kingdom Builders all over the world.

Brian Houston described Andrew Denton, as 'the kind of man every pastor wants in his congregration'.

Millions of dollars in Kingdom Builder donations flowed into the Hillsong Foundation, a charitable fund for which donations are tax deductible. This means donations are effectively subsidised by the government through the taxation system.

Years later serious questions would be raised in parliament and by former Hillsong followers about what happened to the money which flows through Hillsong charities, leaving some donors deeply disillusioned about their sacrificial giving.

A Business that Isn't a Business

Hillsong's constant expansion has always been wrapped in the language of business. Pastors joining the Hillsong brand have had to sign non-disclosure agreements and non-compete agreements, should they leave—a practice used in the world of commerce to protect hard-won territory or clientele. Hillsong Church Australia operates with a board, and there is also a global board, just like a multinational corporation. The church produces an annual report with information on its various activities (though it is not entirely forthcoming with details of payments to senior Hillsong executives, or even a total sum, never mind how much goes to individuals).

Hillsong uses consistent branding on its churches and its products. It has a media department that controls the information flow—and, when things go wrong, it calls in crisis management lawyers, just as a major corporation would.

The very name, 'Hillsong', positions the organisation as being distinct from religion, placing it more in the realm of lifestyle. It is certainly a long way from 'Pentecostal', and a world away from its origins as a 'Christian Life Centre' in the Assemblies of God movement.

In so many ways, Hillsong looks like a business and acts like a business—but it insists it is not a business. And that distinction is the critical factor in Hillsong's success.

If Hillsong were a for-profit 'business', it would be denied the fortune it has received in tax breaks. It would also be denied the ability to operate beyond the power of a regulator, as the special status of some of its charities permits.

The church has a few people to thank for this happy state of affairs. They include smart lawyers, ruthless church lobbyists and, above all, a helpful federal government, which has passed laws delivering dozens of lurks and perks.

Charity status is an earthly treasure for all religions, not only Hillsong. The idea of giving special tax dispensations to churches might have made sense back in the days that the phrase 'poor as a churchmouse' rang true. But what about when the churchmen drive top-of-the-range Audis and Harley-Davidson motorbikes, like Brian Houston? Or live in million-dollar manses? Or, for that matter, wield multibillion-dollar property portfolios, as both the Catholic and Anglican churches do?

In the annals of legal precedent, the case of *Commissioner of Taxation v. Word Investments Ltd*, decided by the High Court of Australia in 2008, was a decisive moment for Hillsong and other Australian religious organisations.

Word Investments was a company closely linked to a Christian missionary organisation called Wycliffe Bible Translators Australia. Wycliffe was involved in various religious activities, including translating the Bible into Indigenous languages. Word Investments was established to raise money through business ventures, including an investment scheme and a funeral home, and gave that money to Wycliffe for its religious purposes.

The Australian Taxation Office (ATO) had refused to grant tax-exempt charity status to Word Investments. One ground for this was that while one of Word's objectives was to proclaim the Christian religion, Word itself did not do this. Rather, all it did was raise money from commercial activities and hand it to other bodies so that they could proclaim the Christian religion.

The ATO submitted that there was no nexus between the profit and the charitable purpose.

The justices of the High Court rejected the ATO's arguments by four to one, opening the way for religious organisations to run profit-making businesses that would be exempt from tax, as long as the profits went to advancing religion.

Word Investments' lawyer—and Australia's foremost charity law expert—Murray Baird, declared that the High Court's decision had 'implications for the Salvation Army running furniture businesses . . . Hillsong selling CDs, the Seventh Day Adventist Church running Sanitarium, making breakfast foods, and the Diabetes Foundation selling used clothing'.

The one dissenting judge, Justice Michael Kirby, wondered aloud about the principle the decision established. He speculated on whether there was any prospect that Word's profits could be used for a 'high lifestyle', such as that enjoyed by US television evangelists.

His musings were prophetic, to say the least.

————

Declaring that your organisation has the aim of advancing religion opens the door to an Aladdin's cave of tax concessions and special deals, all agreed to by the Australian government.

The charities established by Hillsong are exempt from paying income tax. As it is a not-for-profit endeavour, this means that the profits from its multimillion-dollar businesses can accumulate and be invested in further ventures, thereby helping it expand its operations and its influence in other areas. Or what would have been profits—which can't be distributed—can be taken up with expenses that benefit individuals. So, higher private benefits and lower profits. And there is no law or standard that says what is 'reasonable' for these.

Hillsong charities are also exempted from paying the Goods and Services Tax (GST). But the major concession it has is exemption from Fringe Benefits Tax (FBT). This is a financial boon for the church's pastors, because it can dramatically reduce the cash portion of a pastor's salary, on which they pay income tax. The pastor can have a car, housing and their children's education fees paid for as part of their salary package, and pay no tax on these fringe benefits.

Under an ATO tax ruling, all sorts of people can be classed as religious practitioners. Forget the image of a dog-collared clergyman. A religious practitioner can be a layperson performing the work of a minister. Or it can be 'other persons acting in those capacities from time to time'. The definition even extends to students who are doing religious studies or training. In reality, a 'pastor' can be anyone Hillsong says is a pastor.

For Hillsong, this realisation was a true hallelujah moment.

Every Hillsong Church is run not just by a single pastor, but by a husband-and-wife team, both of whom are called pastors. Large churches will have two or three husband-and-wife teams of pastors. Then there are the children of pastors. Pastor Brian and Pastor Bobbie Houston have three children, all of whom at one time held pastor status.

Most of the members of Hillsong's boards are deemed to be pastors. Its creative employees, too, can be called pastors, including those who compose and perform Hillsong music. The decision is up to the Hillsong board. This delivered enormous power to Brian Houston, given that all board members held their positions at the pleasure of the senior pastor, who could remove a board member if he so desired.

This sort of arrangement elevates the senior pastor's power, and is clearly open to cronyism and nepotism. The senior pastor giveth, the senior pastor taketh away.

In the United States, where similar rules apply, the late tel-evangelist Paul Crouch, founder of the giant Trinity Broadcasting Network, reportedly made a habit of ordaining the network's station managers and department heads as ministers so that they could deduct 100 per cent of their housing costs as a par-sonage allowance.

Once you have been named as a pastor, you gain FBT exemp-tions on all manner of salary items. These can relate not only to the pastor, but to their spouse and children. The exemptions even cover live-in housekeepers.

Unlike most other organisations with FBT exemptions, a church's FBT exemption is not subject to any caps. It is there-fore possible for a church to pay a pastor 100 per cent of their salary via FBT salary packaging. This potentially reduces their cash salary to zero and, in theory, would make them eligible for social security benefits.

In practice, most Australian churches pay between 30 per cent and 70 per cent of their clerics' salaries via non-taxable FBT items. Hillsong has not publicly stated what percentage it uses; it is not even known how many pastors it has accredited.

These FBT exemptions count among the great lurks for church organisations. It is more than simply a ruling by the Australian Taxation Office. It exists in legislation passed by the national parliament.

Hillsong's myriad other financial benefits include exemptions from local council rates, and from duty on car purchases and property transfers. Tax-exempt entities are also not required to submit tax returns.

On top of all this, religious institutions in Australia have, under charities laws, been granted extra exemptions that are not available to secular charities. A so-called Basic Religious Charity is not required to lodge a financial report. It does not need to comply with a set of official governance standards that apply to other charities. Nor can the regulator, the ACNC, remove the office holders of any such charity. Being a Basic Religious Charity, in other words, means that you are virtually beyond regulation: you can operate in near-total secrecy. There is nothing you must declare publicly, even though you receive support from the public purse.

The special carve-out for Basic Religious Charities came about when the Labor government was attempting to legislate what ultimately became the *Charities Act 2013*. This was an attempt to better define what a charity was, and to put charities under closer government oversight. But the Gillard/Rudd government of 2010 to 2013 was a minority government; it did not have the numbers in either the House of Representatives or the Senate, and so was vulnerable to pressure from vested interests.

Under intense lobbying by the Catholic Church in particular, the government was persuaded that it was too much to ask small churches, run on the sales of scones and tea and the devotion of volunteers, to comply with the demands of the new regulation. But the Act that ultimately passed through parliament placed no limit on the size or sophistication of the church. Large Catholic and Anglican organisations, with millions of dollars in assets, benefited from the special rules made for 'basic' religious charities.

Hillsong has much to thank them for.

———

Hillsong has been a prolific exploiter of the system set up for charities in Australia. It has had around twenty different charities registered at any one time. These have covered food outlets such as Comma Coffee and Bella Burgers, as well as Hillsong Night School, which charges fees for courses, and Amplified Education Academy.

A Hillsong charity called Community Venues Ltd is the owner of Melbourne's Festival Hall, having acquired it for $23 million.

Another charity, The Trustee for Hillsong International, encompasses a dozen separate entities that drive Hillsong's multimillion-dollar music and broadcast operations. They include Hillsong Music Publishing, the Colour Sisterhood, Hillsong UNITED, and SHOUT! Music Publishing. Hillsong says that the charity holding these entities exists to 'promote the Christian faith'.

HC Australia Property Trust holds and provides properties for the church's ministries in Australia, as well as providing financial support for ministries.

Collectively, the Hillsong entities use every standard tax exemption available to a charity. Some charities operate with near-complete secrecy. Some also have the much-coveted Deductible Gift Recipient (DGR) status, meaning that donations to them are tax-deductible for the donor. This is a direct cost to Australian taxpayers, who effectively subsidise the donation.

Hillsong has various different charitable entities, but the boards that ran them were nearly all identical when Brian Houston ruled the roost.

As well as Hillsong's maze of charities, some senior church figures have their own charities, some of which link to American entities. Brian Houston's son Joel has a charity called Parable Ministries. Hillsong's most senior pastor, Phil Dooley, had his own charity called Live the Adventure Ministries Inc. Nabi Saleh, apart from his Hillsong directorships, is a director of at least three other religious charities registered in Australia, all linked to the wealthy US pastors Kenneth Copeland, Jerry Savelle, Casey Treat and Rick Godwin.

So what guarantees are there that the charity system in Australia works as it should, for both taxpayers and donors?

The system depends on all those pots of money being kept separate from each other, and only being used to support the defined role of the charity. Ultimately, that depends on trust, given the lack of transparency and the impotence of the charities regulator. The various related entities create the perfect conditions for whizzing money around—in, around and between entities.

The Australian charities regulator, the ACNC, was legislated by the Gillard/Rudd Labor administration but was never wanted by the subsequent Coalition government, led by Tony Abbott, who was backed by the religious power of the Catholic Church, in particular. Once in power, Abbott allowed the ACNC to be established—but it took a mealy-mouthed approach, so as to provide the least possible offence to the religions.

It was light-touch regulation at its finest, with charities having the ability to self-report, self-assess and self-monitor—with 'education', rather than compliance and punishment, being the regulator's preferred tool.

Hillsong's rapid early growth was fuelled by successive governments which were prepared to allow special treatment for those in the faith business. After year upon year of untaxed income, Hillsong was ready to go to the next level.

The US was, in a sense, always Brian Houston's spiritual home. Now it was set to become the corporate home to Hillsong and a springboard to yet greater wealth as Brian sought to realise his vision of a truly global church.

The American Reorganisation

In the corporate growth story of Hillsong Inc., mark down 2017 as the year in which the organisation made it really big. This was when the church broke free from its Australian roots to become a fully US-based organisation.

In the new international org chart that emerged, Australia was just one of sixteen countries in which Hillsong was doing business.

Sitting at the very top of the tree was Hillsong Inc., registered in Dallas, Texas. More than 30 US-registered organisations fed into the new mothership, as well as most, if not all, the twenty Australian-registered charities. As well, there were the handful of charities operated by Joel Houston and Nabi Saleh.

The org chart divided the US into three zones: Hillsong West Coast Inc., Hillsong East Coast Inc. and Hillsong Central West Inc. This formal reorganisation of Hillsong's affairs came after years of the church gradually lifting its profile in the United States.

It had opened its first US church in 2010, in New York. Then came Los Angeles in 2013. It added new churches in Arizona, New Jersey and Connecticut. It set up companies for its property portfolio, and for its broadcasting, publishing and music businesses.

From 2017, Hillsong registered more than twenty entities in the United States, most of them set up as religious charities and eligible for similar exemptions to those in Australia. New Hillsong US entities were located in various jurisdictions, but principally Texas. Sometimes, confusingly, entities with the same or similar names were registered in different US states.

When it came to setting up its legal structures, the Houstons did what they always do: they kept things inhouse. The American lawyer they engaged, Stephen Lentz, is the father of Carl Lentz, who had attended a Hillsong training facility in Sydney and struck up a close friendship with Joel Houston. Carl had married a young Australian woman, Laura Betts, whose father was a Pentecostal pastor close to the Houstons.

Carl and Joel had been in Brian's ear about starting a church in New York, and finally it came to pass. And Carl and Joel would be the joint founding pastors. Families who know families. Circles within circles. That's the way it has always been.

This reliance on the ties of friendship and marriage, based on a shared religion, is typical of how the church has always operated, with a small grouping of close royalty around Brian Houston. But these arrangements were to unravel spectacularly later on.

Apart from his Houston connections, lawyer Stephen Lentz also happened to be highly skilled in the technicalities of setting up a church. He had done hundreds of them.

Hillsong's US entities followed the Lentz template. The articles of association stipulated: 'The Corporation shall have no members.' This was a formulation used by many wealthy televangelists. It meant that church attendees were not members, as they might be in other churches—and therefore they had no voting rights. Decision-making power rested with the church's board of directors or church elders—a small group of Houston trusties, most of whom lived thousands of kilometres away from the local action.

Hillsong entities adopted the LLC—limited liability company—structure, another device commonly used by evangelical churches in the United States. Lentz explained the reason in his book *The Business of Church*:

Because we live in a litigious society, it is important to isolate different initiatives that might have high risks. It is first and foremost a containment strategy. We recommend using a single-member limited liability company (LLC) to isolate different church initiatives that are vital to the footprint of the church in its community. Each activity can be vigorously pursued without putting all of the assets of the church at risk.

Barry Bowen is the lead researcher with the Texas-based Trinity Foundation, which has been exposing church fraud for more than 30 years. Bowen has been watching the Hillsong phenomenon unfold in the United States and considers the church's legal structures to be 'dangerous'.

'Jesus once told a parable about two different people constructing houses,' he explains. 'One built on a foundation of stone and the other on sand. When the rains came, the house built on sand collapsed. The foundation was critical for a lasting home. In the parable, the [stone] foundation represented the words of Jesus and obeying them. In a similar manner, Hillsong Church was constructed on a foundation of sand.'

Bowen cites the LLC structure of Hillsong's New York City church and the words of its governing document: 'The limited liability company will be managed by one or more managers.'

'Should the language of business define a church and how it operates?' he asks. 'Stephen Lentz failed to recognise the fatal flaw of church LLCs. There is little, if any, accountability provided for the managers.'

The legal structures used by Hillsong in the United States had the same effect as structures the church had used for decades in Australia. Under Lentz's drafting, Hillsong entities always placed power in the hands of a small number of board members.

They in turn served at the pleasure of Brian Houston, as senior pastor. Ultimately, this gave him the keys to the earthly wealth that sloshed through the Hillsong businesses.

This, finally, was the Hillsong financial machine in full working order—a multinational juggernaut, operating beyond the regulatory regimes of individual nations. It cemented Hillsong's place as a transnational operation, with the missionary purpose of gathering up souls for Jesus at its heart.

However, students of Hillsong's Australian accounts, as reported in the church's publicly available annual reports, noticed one big change around 2017. The accounting entry for the church's music earnings was no longer there.

It turned out this sector had shifted to the United States, the land of infinite millions in the world's largest worship music market, where Hillsong composers—and the church—could make a fortune.

4
APOTHEOSIS

Preparing the Way for Brother Scott

The Pentecostal movement gained its first foothold in an Australian parliament in 2002, when Andrew Evans was elected to the South Australian upper house as a representative of the socially conservative Family First party.

Evans had been the national leader of the Australian Assemblies of God for twenty years, between 1977 and 1997, when the movement was in the throes of an internal power struggle. He was also senior pastor of the Paradise Community Church in Adelaide, one of Australia's largest Pentecostal congregations at the time.

But for all Evans' achievements, it was the heft of the Houstons and Hillsong that produced serious political influence at the national level. Even as Evans entered the South Australian parliament, representing the narrow interests of a small, religious-based party, Hillsong was operating at a national level, bringing Pentecostal influence into the mainstream.

In the same year, 2002, Liberal prime minister John Howard opened Hillsong's new Baulkham Hills centre. It was a sign that this once-fringe religion was too influential to ignore. Hillsong's rise tapped into a rich vein of political support for the Liberal Party, founded on the idea that faith and financial aspiration prospered side by side in the suburbs of Australia's cities.

The year 2004 was a political turning point for Hillsong. Treasurer Peter Costello attended the organisation's annual convention, which had transformed from being a simple gathering of Pentecostal church members into a major new force in the nation's affairs. Costello—a product of Melbourne's Carey Baptist Grammar School and the brother of a prominent Baptist minister, Tim Costello—delivered an address titled 'The Moral Decay of Australia', in which he invoked the Judeo-Christian-Western tradition and lamented that few could recite the Ten Commandments, despite them being 'the foundation of our law and our society'.

This was also the year a Hillsong candidate made it into the federal parliament. Louise Markus, a social worker and a long-term Hillsong attendee, gained Liberal Party preselection and won the seat of Greenway in the election that delivered Howard's government a fourth term.

Markus had been working as a manager of Hillsong community outreach services at Emerge Family Counselling and Enterprise Centre in the lower-socio-economic Sydney area of Blacktown. The centre assisted people with drug and alcohol addiction, and helped those in need to find jobs and housing. It also provided advice on how to set up a business.

Commentators saw Markus as representative of Howard's 'aspirationals'—ordinary suburban folk who just wanted to build a better life for their families, and felt that the Coalition would be their best supporters in this aim. She saw her mission as helping families own their own homes, run their own businesses, educate their children, be safe in their communities and 'be able to get home at a reasonable hour to spend time with their families and to enjoy the quality of life they have worked so hard to achieve'.

When she took her seat in parliament, Markus offered effusive praise for her Hillsong leaders. 'Over the last twenty-one years, I have been blessed to sit under the teaching and leadership of Pastors Brian and Bobbie Houston,' she said. 'Their passion and love for God and for people are unmatched. They have taught me to live life "large", to live for a larger cause. We were not placed on this planet to serve self-interest but to serve the interests of others. We are indeed blessed to be a blessing.'

Brian Houston later cited Louise Markus's election to the government as an example of Hillsong's growing influence in the 'seven spheres' that run society.

'Hillsong Church has so many leaders in all of those various spheres . . . and it inspires me because I believe it's what we're called to do, to reach and influence this world by raising and empowering people to lead and impact in every sphere of life,' he said. 'And every time [Markus] won an election in various ways, that was a miracle. It was against the odds and, when she first came to talk to me, she was just a lovely young lady who worked in our Hillsong CityCare. And she was just faithful and did social work. And so she came to me and told me that she wanted to stand for politics and stand for parliament, federal parliament, but it was in a seat where her party had never, ever won in the whole history of that electorate, more than fifty years. Not even once. So she's telling me this, this sweet Louise—and I'll be honest with you, I was thinking, "You haven't got a hope." I was saying all the right things. I was encouraging her, but on the inside I'm thinking, "Fat chance." Well, I'm glad that God knew more than I know.'

Markus acknowledged in her first speech to parliament that her campaign—in a seat that had in fact only been created in 1984—could not have happened without 'scores of new members and supporters who came out of the woodwork'. And from among the Liberal Party officials who helped her campaign, she singled out one for special praise: 'I particularly want to acknowledge Scott Morrison, the State Director of the New South Wales Liberal Party, whose counsel, support, advice and commitment were absolutely critical to the outcome,' she told the House of Representatives in her maiden speech.

Newspaper reports of the day painted an illuminating picture of the then 36-year-old state director, Morrison, as a controlling, religiously driven operator. Said the *Sydney Morning Herald*:

You might have thought someone standing for such a marginal seat would want all the media attention he or she could get, but the Liberals' State Director, Scott Morrison, refused to let the *Herald* talk to her. He said she would do 'local media first'.

Instead Morrison, himself a man of 'strong religious views', launched into a pitch for the type of 'faith-based programs' that Hillsong had established to address social problems.

'In the [United] States there is an increasing tendency of governments—particularly the Bush Government—to get behind what are called faith-based programs,' [Morrison] enthused.

'That is where governments start to lift the constraints on the Noffses and the Bill Crewses and others, to enable them to really help people, beyond just the material, and give them life advice which involves faith. Those programs, I understand, have had some great success.'

The up-and-coming Liberal star was referring to the White House's Faith-Based and Community Initiative, established by President George W. Bush in 2001. The program aimed to give faith-based groups a greater role in delivering social services, alongside secular organisations, and a share of federal government funds to do so. It was created through the first executive order signed by the new president, who said it would make it possible for all organisations, faith-based or secular, to compete 'on a level playing field'.

The *Herald* also noted that Hillsong's Leigh Coleman, who was Louise Markus's boss at Emerge and a mentor to Scott Morrison, would not permit her to speak with the media.

Three years later it was campaign mastermind Scott Morrison's turn to take a seat in the federal parliament, as the member for

Sydney's southern beaches seat of Cook. He would later have ample opportunity, which he took, to channel government funds to faith-based services.

The Houston Candidate

Scott Morrison and Brian Houston, Australia's religious power duo, had soaring careers that ran in parallel and crossed over many times. Both men reached their peak when Morrison was prime minister, before both collapsed suddenly, just weeks apart.

Initially, Morrison made his way into politics through the patronage of another Christian Liberal politician, Bruce Baird, the patriarch of a family that has had a large impact on Australian public life.

Morrison crossed paths with Baird when both worked at Tourism Australia. Baird then entered the federal parliament as the member for Cook in 1998. When it came time for him to move on, Baird gave Morrison a quiet call, alerting him to the possibility that he might take over his seat.

Baird was certain Morrison was the man for the job, in what was a hotly contested preselection race. 'He is a person of faith and it is not a pretend faith,' Baird told the Christian radio station Hope. 'He's a very strong family man. I know he's concerned about religious freedom.' And there was more, a sense even of divine destiny: 'It's also true to say that my wife, Judy, believed [Morrison] was called by God to replace me. That's known within our family.'

The Bairds' certainty that Morrison was called by God matched Morrison's own calling, apparently separate, from the

Holy Spirit. By one account, the first occasion was around the year 2000, when Baptist minister Brian Stewart recalls Morrison telling him, as they walked from their cars to a birthday celebration, that God had told him he would be prime minister one day. This coincides with the period that Morrison attended Hillsong's city church in Sydney, then under the control of Brian Houston.

In the years prior to the 2007 federal election, Morrison told a senior Hillsong pastor, Joel A'Bell, that God had chosen him to be prime minister one day, as A'Bell later revealed. And so when Morrison arrived in parliament, it appears he had a fully formed view of himself as a Christian politician with a destiny to lead—or perhaps better *run*—the country.

For those who hadn't been paying attention to his work with Louise Markus, Morrison made his Christian calling and his religious indebtedness very clear in his first speech to parliament in 2008. In it he paid generous tribute to pastors Brian Houston and Leigh Coleman for the influence they had had on his life.

'Australia is not a secular country—it is a free country,' he said, raising a distinction which perhaps few fully appreciated at the time. 'This is a nation where you have the freedom to follow any belief system you choose. Secularism is just one. It has no greater claim than any other on our society. As US Senator Joe Lieberman said, the Constitution guarantees freedom of religion, not from religion. I believe the same is true in this country.

'So what values do I derive from my faith? My answer comes from Jeremiah, chapter 9:24: "I am the Lord who exercises loving-kindness, justice and righteousness on earth; for I delight in these things, declares the Lord."'

In the same speech, he told, for the first time to a national audience, the story of the 'miracle' birth of his and Jenny's daughter Abbey, after years of failed IVF attempts, citing a set of numbers which pointed to the biblical Day of Pentecost. 'After fourteen years of bitter disappointments, God remembered [Jenny's] faithfulness and blessed us with our miracle child, Abbey Rose, on the seventh of the seventh of the seventh,' he said, and he dedicated his first parliamentary address to his daughter.

Morrison's speech also contained a little-reported and little-understood reference to the historical figure William Wilberforce. While the secular world knows Wilberforce for his role in ending the British slave trade in the late 1700s and early 1800s, devout Christians have a completely different understanding of his life. In the world of Christian evangelism, Wilberforce is a hero because he was a politician who used his influence within the British government to light the flame of Christianity in Australia. Morrison hailed him as a man who stood for the 'immutable truths and principles of the Christian faith', and who had transformed his nation and the world.

There are tomes devoted to the 'real story' of the British parliamentarian, who was a leading light of the so-called Clapham Sect, a grouping of evangelical Christian MPs also known as 'The Saints', who gathered in houses around the common in Clapham, in south-west London. Author and blogger Kurt Mahlburg has written of Wilberforce's role in Christianising the young colony of Australia in his book *Great Southland Revival*.

According to Mahlburg, 'contrary to popular mythology', Australia's founding was 'not a triumph of secularism', nor a tale of mere vice and ungodliness. Australia, he writes, was a 'product of revival': 'The First Fleet set sail from a Britain profoundly reformed by the Great Awakening, and ready to greet the dawn of the Second Great Awakening.'

David Furse-Roberts, a research fellow at the Liberal Party's Menzies Research Centre, has written of the 'profound imprint' Wilberforce's combination of 'evangelical Christianity and humane liberalism' had on the formation of modern Australia. 'While Wilberforce's liberal credentials were less than perfect, with his opposition to free religious debate and the rights of trade unions, his Evangelicalism nonetheless helped craft a liberalism that renounced slavery, affirmed the dignity of all people and dared to dream of improvement,' he wrote in the politically conservative *Spectator* magazine.

Scott Morrison's homage to Wilberforce, the Christian evangelist, was a clear indication of how the new federal MP saw the role of religion in politics. It was also an example of Morrison's ability to speak to two audiences at once: the secular and the religious. But to really know what he meant, you had to understand the code. And, perhaps luckily for Morrison, very few did.

———

It wasn't just God who was on Scott Morrison's side—so were the godly.

Morrison's first five years in the federal parliament were spent in opposition. Not being in government meant that no one was paying much attention to him—except, that is, for those who wanted to sponsor the godly to wield power.

In 2011 Morrison noted on his parliamentary register of interests that he had received free flights to the United States from an organisation called the Oceania Fellowship. This organisation had also given him a seat at the 2011 US National Prayer Breakfast, the big-ticket annual event hosted by the incumbent president (Barack Obama, at the time) and which attracted both politicians and people of faith.

A key figure in the Oceania Fellowship was Jock Cameron, a stalwart religious influencer who worked behind the scenes to build religious connections within the Australia parliament. One of those initiatives was Australia's own National Prayer Breakfast, modelled directly on the US event.

However, of all the Christian influences on Morrison, none was greater than Pastor Brian Houston. Morrison looked to Houston as his mentor and adviser. On Morrison's own telling of their history, it was Houston who told Morrison, years before he was anywhere near the prime minister's office, that he should use what God had put 'in his hand'. Houston's words to the politician are rich in Biblical meaning, and cast Morrison as a Moses figure—one to whom God had given special powers.

Exodus 4 records that the Lord asked Moses: 'What is that in your hand?' The chapter continues:

He said, 'A rod.' And He said, 'Cast it on the ground.' So he cast it on the ground, and it became a serpent; and Moses fled from it. But the Lord said to Moses, 'Put out your hand and catch it by the tail'—so he put out his hand and caught it, and it became a staff in his hand.

This text illustrates an important principle: Moses used what God had put in his hand. Moses' years of tending sheep were not useless. Those years had put into Moses' hand things he could use for God's glory.

Like much in the relationship between the politician, Scott Morrison, and the pastor, Brian Houston, many of their communications are secret or soaked in impenetrable Christianese.

As Scott Morrison ascended through the coalition ranks, from backbencher to cabinet minister and Treasurer, this must surely have been God's plan at work.

The timing aligned magnificently with Brian Houston's publicly expressed belief that the godly should wield influence in the seven key spheres of society.

With the aid of prayers from fellow Pentecostal believer Coalition MP Stuart Robert, Morrison emerged as the successor to prime minister Malcolm Turnbull.

Morrison, staff in hand, had claimed the ultimate prize.

A Time of Miracles

When Prime Minister Scott Morrison led his Coalition government to victory in the 2019 election, defeating Bill Shorten, whose triumph the secular seers had falsely predicted, the PM, almost Lazarus-like, proclaimed his win a miracle. And with that, Morrison marked himself as the man whom God had delivered into the prime ministership.

'I have always believed in miracles,' a suddenly powered-up Morrison announced, hitting the word *always*, as the cheers rose from the throng of Liberal Party supporters, who perhaps couldn't quite believe the unlikely win themselves. Behind the re-elected prime minister, Jenny Morrison mouthed a very obvious 'Yes!' to her husband's words.

The secular world talks about miracles too. They are things that happen against the odds. It's a word used all the time. Australians with a passing interest in politics might have taken Morrison's words as an expression of exuberance and nothing more.

But to a Christian ear the word *miracle* has another tone. It is not only a profession of absolute faith in God, it is an overt acceptance that God has directed the course of events. And to a Pentecostal ear, it is something different again: a direct reference to the day of the Pentecost and a signal that Morrison was very much part of God's plan for these confused times. 'I believe in miracles,' Bobbie Houston tweeted a year later as a statement of her very being.

It was Morrison at his Christian dog-whistling best, broadcasting and narrowcasting at the same time. No one really twigged at the time—least of all Australia's political journalists—but the miracles, signs of God, demons, Satan and heavenly interventions which abound in Morrison's world of Pentecostal Christianity were about to take centre stage in Australian public life.

Over Morrison's three and a half years in the Lodge, he became less and less inhibited about his religion. For those watching closely, the outline of a radically religious prime minister gradually became clear. The master illusionist felt empowered to use what God had put in his hand.

Privately, Morrison—although he looked the very image of the daggy suburban dad—was pondering the role God had assigned him.

How do we know this?

After leaving office, Morrison told a congregation at former tennis champion Margaret Court's Pentecostal church, the Victory Life Centre in Perth, that he 'often' reflected on the story of Joshua and the walls of Jericho when he was prime minister. 'On the day, in fact, when I became prime minister,' he said. The thought of God watching over him had calmed him in his anxious moments.

In the Old Testament narrative, Joshua is leading an army, trying to take the city of Jericho. God gives him a strategy which sounds ridiculous to non-believers. The soldiers he commands must march around the city every day for six days. On the seventh day they must march around the walls seven times, after which priests should raise their trumpets. The people of Jericho, by this point, are standing on the walls and jeering. When the trumpets sound, the walls fall down. Then Joshua's army enter and take the city.

Joshua and the soldiers did something that made no sense, but they weren't afraid to look foolish in honouring God. In return, God honoured them and they won the physical battle. The message—very common among devout Christians—is not to be afraid to look like a fool when serving Christ.

Morrison had played the game God asked, being unafraid to follow God's instructions, and now the walls had come down and the physical city was his for the taking.

A second inference of the story is that Joshua was unsure of his abilities, having just inherited the role of leader from Moses, who had led the Israelites out of Egypt. Joshua's job was to lead his people across the Jordan River into Canaan and take back the land God had promised Abraham.

Just weeks after he won the 2019 election, Morrison appeared on stage with Brian Houston at Hillsong's 2019 annual conference. For those who had missed the 'miracle' reference on election night, Morrison obliged with more.

The newly re-elected PM offered prayers for 'veterans who are doing it tough', for young people and 'the curse of suicide', for people suffering from mental health, for the 'remote Indigenous', for families and people who 'live with disabilities, physical disabilities, intellectual disabilities'. Finally, Morrison wanted to pray for the end of the drought.

It was quite the list of concerns. Morrison was showing great compassion—but why was he leaving serious public policy issues and the impacts of climate change to God to handle, when he might have empowered experts and the droves of federal government employees?

Before leaving the stage, Morrison gave his word to the Hillsong Conference that there would be legislation to protect religious freedom, as his mentor Brian Houston wanted. There was no pat on the head for the prime minister, but there was huge applause, whoops and cheers from the 20,000 Hillsongers packed into the stadium.

Later that year, Morrison put it all on the line for his mentor when the pastor hoped to attend a White House state dinner.

Morrison pushed unsuccessfully for Brian Houston to be included on the official guest list for the reception hosted by Donald Trump during Morrison's first visit to the United States as prime minister. *The Wall Street Journal* broke the story that Morrison had been 'determined' to have Houston included, and that there had been several rounds of discussions between the governments before the White House vetoed the idea.

Morrison refused to confirm this for several months, dismissing it as gossip. 'I'm not going to go into the habit of just because one journalist somewhere in the world talks to someone who won't put their name to it, and all of a sudden apparently we've got to play twenty questions,' he told an interviewer. 'That's just not how I'm going to operate. If people have an established source who's prepared to put their names to things, well, that's a different matter.'

Only later did he finally confirm the story during a radio interview, although he ducked the central reason Houston was knocked back: the pastor was under police investigation at the time for allegedly concealing the child sex crimes committed by his late father.

———

The Covid-19 pandemic brought more public displays of Morrison's belief in the power of the supernatural to fix earthly problems.

In the early weeks of the pandemic, he spoke to an online prayer group, asking that people pray for everyone affected by Covid. 'Pray for the premiers and chief ministers who have joined me in the national cabinet,' he began. 'It is a moment like when Moses looked out to sea, held up his staff and led people to the promised land. As a prime minister I have to take my decisions on the basis of very strong advice and exercise the best judgement I possibly can, and my faith gives me enormous encouragement in how I can make those decisions and try to do that the best way I can.'

There it was again: Morrison as Moses with his staff in his hand, just as Brian Houston had foreseen. It was the staff of God which turned into a serpent as a sign of Moses' direct relationship with God. That was the same staff that would later part the Red Sea, as well as strike a rock and see water pour forth.

Morrison carried on, sharing Biblical verses, specifically from Isaiah 61:4, which says: 'They shall build up the ancient ruins; they shall raise up the former devastations; they shall repair the ruined cities, the devastations of many generations.'

'That's a prophecy over our country, I believe,' he told the gathering, 'and you will raise up the age-old foundations; you will be called repairer of broken walls, and a restorer of streets with dwellings. I pray that we will be a restorer of streets, with people in them, businesses open again, Australians going about their lives again, returning to their jobs, returning to their livelihoods, returning to normal times in our schools so children can learn and that we can get to the other side of this.'

He told the Nine Network's *60 Minutes* that, as he'd campaigned for re-election, he had 'worn down the carpet beside my bed praying for all those souls' affected by Covid.

———

In April 2021 Scott Morrison presented himself at Australian Pentecostalism's biggest event, the biennial conference of the Australian Christian Churches (ACC), held on the Gold Coast.

This was not an official prime ministerial function. Morrison, the Pentecostal man, was away from the public gaze—or so he thought—when he delivered an off-the-cuff address to the hundreds of Pentecostal pastors who had gathered from across the country. Unfortunately for Morrison—a man who normally loved to have a camera around—someone recorded his every word.

Here was Morrison unplugged. As prime minister, he often appeared defensive and agitated in public, as though he wore an ill-fitting mask. Questions from journalists seeking account-ability put him on edge. In the run-up to the ACC conference he had endured intense pressure over the Covid vaccination rollout, with safety questions emerging over the AstraZeneca vaccine.

That was one of the two approved vaccines in Australia, and the one which was in ready supply. But the government's vaccine experts, the Australian Technical Advisory Group on Immuni-sation—known as ATAGI—had recommended heavy restrictions on the use of AstraZeneca, effectively knocking out the govern-ment's strategy. ATAGI's move had also led to an open season of attacks on Morrison himself.

His enemies had been snapping at his heels. On this night, however, Morrison was among friends. All inhibitions were gone. He was in the embrace of his religious tribe.

Morrison made his way onto the stage as a conquering hero returning from the secular lands. Was he simply a Pentecostal believer? Or was he the leader of the Australian government?

It was, as was often the case, a blend of the two. The prime minister/believer-in-chief proceeded to deliver what sounded like a word salad to outsiders, but it made complete sense to the audience, and marked him out as a Pentecostal man to his core.

The PM's opening words let everyone know he was present as their brother.

'The Great Southern Land of the Holy Spirit,' he began, referring to the country he governed, but using an Australian Pentecostal term. This referred to the idea that Australia has been chosen as the place for the great end times revival that would impact all nations. His words evoked the legend of Smith Wigglesworth, the English plumber who in the early 1900s had foreseen a leading role for Australian Pentecostalism in shaping the future.

Morrison brought news, in words that he knew his fellow Pentecostal believers would appreciate, about the outside world and how things were unfolding out there. It emerged as a case of him—and his audience—versus the outside world.

First he nodded to the presence of two other Pentecostal members of parliament—'my brothers', as Morrison called them—the Gold Coast MP Stuart Robert and the newly arrived Western Australian senator Matt O'Sullivan, who, Morrison said, had joined 'our band of Christian believers in Canberra'.

The star in the audience, though, was Brian Houston—the biggest name in Australian Pentecostalism and perhaps the main reason for Morrison making this unpublicised and off-the-book visit. For him the prime minister had the warmest of words: 'Just pay you honour, mate,' he said, picking out Brian and Bobbie Houston in the crowd.

Morrison related how seeing a picture of a soaring eagle in a gallery owned by a photographer and fellow Christian, Ken Duncan, had spurred him on during the 2019 election campaign. Morrison interpreted the photograph as a message from God that he should push on against the growing fatigue and pessimism of his apparently doomed campaign:

'I must admit, I was saying to myself, "Where are you? Where are you? I'd like a reminder, if that's okay,"' he said of his attempts to find God, who had apparently deserted him. 'And I walked into [Ken Duncan's] gallery and there, right in front of me, was the biggest picture of a soaring eagle that I could imagine.' He said it reminded him of Isaiah 40:31: 'But those who hope in the Lord will renew their strength. They will soar on wings like eagles; they will run and not grow weary, they will walk and not be faint.' That photograph from Ken Duncan's gallery ended up enjoying pride of place in the prime minister's Canberra office.

Surely it could only be a coincidence that Brian Houston is known in Pentecostal circles by his nickname, 'the Eagle'.

Morrison let his friends in on another secret. He had brought the healing power of God into the lives of people who had been devastated by natural disasters, although they had no idea what he was doing: 'I've been in evacuation centres where people thought I was just giving someone a hug and I was praying. And putting my hands on people in various places, laying hands on them and praying in various situations.'

As his audience well understood, the practice of the laying on of hands is a form of spiritual healing common among

Pentecostalists. Those who knew the code were left in no doubt that Morrison was and is central to God's plan.

He peppered his address with the kind of Christianese you would hear in any Hillsong sermon. Going through a bad time would be a difficult 'season'. Morrison had a few things 'on my heart' that he wanted to talk about. Several times he invoked the phrase 'for such a time as this'. The words are drawn from the book of Esther and are a kind of shorthand for the desperate times we live in, where an individual anointed by God plays a key role in staving off disaster.

In other references he painted a very strong picture, cumulatively, of a man convinced he has been anointed by God to prepare the secular world for God's kingdom on earth.

In the presence of Australia's Pentecostal elite, Scott Morrison could not have been clearer about where he stood and, as he saw it, the primacy of God over government. But what no one knew was that, in the days coinciding with his destiny-soaked Pentecostal appearance, Morrison had secretly had himself appointed to lead three government ministries. And those were in addition to two other ministries he had previously assumed.

On 15 April, six days before his Gold Coast address, Morrison had made himself the Minister for Industry, Science, Energy and Resources (a single ministry). The day after his Pentecostal address, 22 April, he sent a letter to Governor-General David Hurley recommending he be appointed to administer two further departments, Treasury and Home Affairs—in the latter case, giving himself power over Australia's security agencies.

A year before, he had appointed himself Minister for Health as well as Finance Minister, citing the Covid-19 crisis as his rationale. But now his official letters to the governor-general, which were later obtained under freedom-of-information laws by *The Guardian*, gave no reason whatsoever for his appointment to these three new ministries.

In total, Morrison was now secretly in charge of five government departments, as well as being prime minister. The time of his address to the Pentecostal faithful marked the last of his moves to secretly take to himself considerable government powers.

Morrison, to be sure, was now in a world removed as he gave himself more and more powers.

———

In 2019, as they headed down to Canberra for the annual National Prayer Breakfast, one of Hillsong's leading power couples, Donna and Stephen Crouch, declared it an 'inspiring moment' to gather in the Great Hall of Parliament House with leaders and people of faith.

'To have the Hon. Scott Morrison MP, Prime Minister of Australia and the Hon. Anthony Albanese MP, Leader of the Opposition, and the Governor-General of Australia, the Hon. David Hurley, all involved is stunning,' they said. 'Unity is a Jesus thing. Thank you to the Parliamentary Christian Fellowship. Whatever else prayer might be, it is an act of humility. There is something beautiful and noble about our leaders acknowledging they are not "top dog" in the universe—expressing out loud that they are accountable to Something higher than themselves and that, despite their commitment to using every faculty of human reason, they could do with some outside assistance.'

For Donna and Stephen Crouch, Morrison was the main man.

And Morrison's main man was Brian Houston, the window cleaner from small-town New Zealand who had become a global phenomenon and senior pastor to the Crouches. In Morrison's style of Pentecostalism, all roads led to Houston.

As it happened, Morrison's local Pentecostal church was not Hillsong, but it might as well have been. Shirelive was 'planted' by Pastor Michael Murphy, who had been a Hillsong pastor. The church had adopted the Hillsong formula, as had other large Pentecostal churches across Australia.

In Perth, for example, the popular Globalheart Church had been set up by former Hillsong senior pastors Gerard and Sue Keehan. The Keehan team had 'planted' the London Christian Life Centre, which later became Hillsong London, before they arrived in Perth.

All around the country at this time, Hillsong was at its peak—as was the influence of Pentecostalism in Scott Morrison's Liberal Party.

Brian's Big Day

Who would ever have imagined that a boy from a state-owned house in Lower Hutt, New Zealand, would one day be striding into the White House to pray with the President of the United States of America? That must surely be proof that God's plan of prosperity for believers is real—even if the president in question,

Donald Trump, had made a mockery of what it meant to be a Christian.

Yes, December 2019 brought one of the sweetest moments in the Life of Brian. The pastor from down under had made it all the way to the Cabinet Room of the White House, where he was among a group of American 'worship leaders' who attended a 'faith briefing' with the vice president, Mike Pence.

The 40 or so worship leaders held what became a raucous and rapturous meeting, with Pence, a conservative evangelical Christian, popping in briefly. There was an outpouring of joy as guitar-strumming led the group into an impromptu gospel music performance. The faith leaders swayed in unison, their palms open and raised to the heavens, and they whooped in ecstasy.

Next came the big moment. The group was shepherded into the Oval Office for a photo opportunity with Donald Trump himself. Houston managed to gain pole position, at the right hand of the president and just one row back. It was a photograph that sent a powerful message to the broader Pentecostal world.

———

After the historic meeting in the Oval Office, a video message from Brian Houston was posted to social media. Houston had well over half a million Twitter and Instagram followers. However, this video message was posted not by Houston but by the White House, a sign that any meeting with Donald Trump was, above all, a transaction from which Trump planned to benefit.

For the official video, Houston was filmed inside the White House, framed by the United States flag and by the dark-blue presidential flag, and accompanied by the president's coat of arms.

'Well, what an honour to be standing in the White House, in the Cabinet Room, and to have just had the chance to pray for President Trump,' Houston began. 'I do, as an Australian, really believe that we need a strong America in the world, and when America is strong the world is a better place.

'What a great opportunity it has been to see some of the initiatives that are happening to help freedom of religion, and to just see, generally, the great spirit in the White House where people are optimistic about the future.

'Praise God for the opportunity.'

Having sung for his supper, Houston made a separate video message for his followers, this time shot in the grounds of the White House. He added the hashtag: '#neversaynever'.

'Well, here I am at the White House. Never say never. It was a great honour of course to have had the chance to go into the Cabinet Room, even into the Oval Office, and to pray for the President of the United States of America. To me it's not about the politics. It's about the position, and a significant man, like the President of the United States, can do with all the prayer we can possibly give him.'

Houston was clearly on a high. And why not? Having bathed in the glow of Trump's fame and presidential power, the pastor was surely at the summit of his career. With Houston's friend and spiritual mentee, Scott Morrison, in the Lodge in Canberra, and that great friend of the evangelical movement Donald Trump in the White House, could Christian influence on government in the two nations be any greater?

Houston was also having the last laugh, at the expense of those who had prevented him from accompanying Scott Morrison to a state dinner at the White House two months before. Morrison had been determined to secure an invitation for his close friend, but as mentioned earlier Houston was at the time under police investigation in Australia for allegedly concealing the sex abuse crimes of his father.

'Never say never' may have been an oblique reference to his failure to retain that invitation, but clearly the cloud that hung over Frank Houston posed no problems for Pence or Trump. Nor was it, apparently, an issue for Trump's closest evangelical adviser, Florida pastor Paula White, who had organised the visit.

The picture of Brian Houston in a huddle around President Donald Trump spoke volumes about where the Hillsong pastor had landed after years of associating with America's Christian right as he expanded the Hillsong enterprise.

The photo was also a tableau of America's pastor power. Dr Andy Rowell, a professor at Bethel Seminary in Minneapolis, analysed the identities of the 40 or so worship leaders who attended the Trump meeting, to understand the influence of those who had gathered.

Leading the roster was the permanently blonde and power-suited Paula White. It takes a special Christian spirit to see the value in a character like Donald Trump, and Pastor Paula White clearly has that. A decade earlier, she had been one of the targets of Senator Chuck Grassley's inquiry into US televangelists. That inquiry revealed that White's organisation required employees to sign a confidentiality agreement that prevented them from ever discussing anything about her religious organisation.

A fierce supporter of Israel, White had delivered the opening prayer at Trump's 2017 inauguration. She had hosted a Political Action Committee (PAC) fundraiser at Trump's Mar-a-Lago resort in Florida. She had a condo in Trump Tower.

The other pastors included Jentezen Franklin, a 60-something celebrity televangelist and author who is the senior pastor of a 14,000-strong megachurch based in Gainesville, Georgia. Franklin became Trump's unofficial evangelical adviser and featured in Trump campaign events, spruiking the evangelical priorities of pro-life initiatives, religious freedom and the appointment of conservative judges. Franklin was no stranger to Brian Houston: he has been a regular speaker at Hillsong's big-bash annual conferences in Sydney, billed as a 'much-loved and long-standing friend' of the church.

Andy Rowell's analysis shows that the largest contingent of pastors that day came from the evangelical charismatic megachurch known as Bethel Church, led by Pastor Bill Johnson. (Bethel Church is unrelated to Rowell's Bethel Seminary.) Pastor Johnson had that very year featured as the headline act at Hillsong's annual conference, the same conference at which Scott Morrison had shared the stage with Brian Houston.

Johnson and his Bethel Church are best known for their association with the breakout Pentecostal Christian movement known as the New Apostolic Reformation, which seeks to transform society by conquering the Seven Mountains of influence.

The leader of the Bethel Church publicly argued the case to vote for Trump in both 2016 and 2020; he said abortion, the welfare system, same-sex marriage, socialism, political correctness and globalisation were all contrary to God's will—a set of targets not dissimilar to Scott Morrison's own preoccupations as a social conservative politician.

Rowell also identified Sean Feucht, a Christian singer-songwriter who ran as a Republican candidate in California in 2020 on a hardline right-to-life platform, and who attracted criticism by holding a live performance at the height of the Covid-19 outbreak. He refers to Houston reverently as 'the boss, the eagle, the legend'.

What has been the attraction of Houston to American evangelists and politicians alike?

'Brian Houston is among the top twenty most well-known pastors in the world,' explains Rowell, who was a pastor from 1999 to 2005, before becoming a teacher of trainee pastors. 'Hillsong music is extremely popular. It's used in a huge number of churches in the US. They look at Houston and see a handsome guy who is a great speaker, a guy who has been really successful, an entrepreneur with some really cool, dynamic churches. So Brian Houston, to them, is someone who is cool. They would want to pick his brains about what's happening in Australia and about what's happening in the world.'

Yet Rowell says Houston was 'naive' to be pictured with Donald Trump.

'The Trump administration's strategy is to use these worship leaders, who have big Instagram followings, to amplify what

Trump is doing for evangelicals. But it should be sobering for Houston and others to realise that they are being used to boost President Trump's popularity,' he says.

'I don't think pastors like Brian Houston know the world of politics and issues so well. The connections are more about individual morality and their fear of creeping secularism. The emphasis of these conservative politicians and pastors is to protect religious freedoms and to get rid of government regulation. They see the poor as this lower class of people who can't be helped and who need to work harder. They equate helping the poor with communism or socialism.'

That equation was summed up eloquently by a pro-Trump pastor from Texas named Ed Young, who distilled the electoral choice facing Americans into a simple binary: 'Will we continue to be a republic under God? Or will we slouch toward Godless socialism?'

Rowell also highlights 'religious freedom'. It is the very phrase Houston used in his social media message after meeting with Trump in December 2019. He had used the same term when he was joined on stage by Prime Minister Morrison at Hillsong's conference earlier that year. The issue was so important to Houston that he made Morrison pledge, in front of 20,000 people, to implement it in legislation.

And Morrison tried his hardest to do so, even if it was the last thing he did as prime minister.

A Hero among Donald Trump's Republicans

Brian Houston insisted, in his video statement after leaving the White House, that meeting President Trump had been 'not about the politics, it's about the position'. Yet, as he no doubt under-stood, the evangelical Christian project and the Republican Party were at that point utterly intertwined.

In America, the idea of religious freedom or religious liberty has been a rallying cry for decades. Any party advocating small government is a natural ally for a religious movement seeking to establish a kingdom of God on Earth. Even better would be a political party which advocated for no government at all—a position Trump's Republican backers favoured. If you are going to pay a tax on your income, then it's better that it be a tithe paid to the church, rather than going in support of a secular state that, they say, wishes to curtail your religious freedom.

Where and when did all this begin?

The marriage of Big Politics, Big Religion and Big Money can be traced back to the 1930s and the founding of an organisation called The Family (or The Fellowship), which aimed to promote theocratic capitalist power in Washington by quietly enlisting up-and-coming politicians and businessmen to its cause.

The Fellowship is best known for staging the annual National Prayer Breakfast in Washington, which the president tradition-ally attends. (As we saw earlier, Scott Morrison, at the time a Liberal Party opposition member, attended the National Prayer Breakfast in 2011.)

Investigative reporter Jeff Sharlet, who once lived inside a Fellowship-owned residence, described in his book *The Family: The Secret Fundamentalism at the Heart of American Power* the movement's philosophy as 'elite fundamentalism' and depicted an organisation obsessive about political power and wealth, and stridently opposed to labour unions. Members believed that laissez-faire economics was God's will.

Sharlet's account of life inside the 'frat house for Jesus', as it was derisively known, argued that the theological teaching of instant forgiveness had given powerful men a convenient means of escaping the consequences of their misdeeds or crimes. It had enabled them to avoid being made accountable for their actions.

The Fellowship sought to integrate faith into politics, more so than into a particular political party. However, in the 1970s, powerful religious men, such as the Baptist minister Reverend Jerry Falwell, overtly sought to colonise the Republican Party for their own political purposes. Falwell's Moral Majority movement campaigned on traditional family values. It capitalised on religious unease about the legalisation of abortion as a result of the US Supreme Court's *Roe v. Wade* decision in 1973.

Falwell was credited with delivering two-thirds of the white evangelical vote to Ronald Reagan during the 1980 presidential election. According to the incumbent president, the Democratic Party's Jimmy Carter, 'that autumn [1980] a group headed by Jerry Falwell purchased $10 million in commercials on southern radio and TV to brand me as a traitor to the South and no longer a Christian'.

Accounts differ, but on one credible analysis, evangelical Christians were galvanised by another hot-button issue, which also came along in the years after *Roe v. Wade*. Simmering away in the background was the issue of racial segregation and the right of a religious-run organisation to employ or educate whomever they deemed suitable, and to exclude others as they saw fit.

The US Supreme Court ruled in 1983 that the Internal Revenue Service could deny a Christian university, the Bob Jones University, its tax-exempt status because it excluded Black students.

This court ruling became a signal to Christian politicians about what might happen in the future if the government were permitted to interfere in the affairs of evangelical institutions. And religious campaigners now had their issue: religious freedom.

The Republican Party was happy to prosecute it. And there was a growing evangelical population willing to be mobilised at the ballot box. According to the Pew Research Center, white evangelical Protestants, who constitute one in every five voters, have consistently been among the strongest supporters of Republican candidates. They supported Donald Trump by a margin of 77 per cent to 16 per cent in the 2016 election. White evangelical voters made up a much greater share of Trump's voters (34 per cent) than Democratic candidate Hillary Clinton's (7 per cent) in the 2016 presidential election.

Pew's research also shows that Trump's electoral performance among white evangelicals was even stronger in 2020 than in 2016, with Trump having delivered on the issues of abortion and religious freedom.

It was proof that the religious right had achieved its aim to change the United States by entwining itself utterly with the Republican Party—a lesson hardly lost on Brian Houston, ambitious to have God-ordained global impact.

———

There are many individuals who paved the way for Brian Houston to end up in the White House that day as an ally of, and a spruiker for, the Trump administration.

Houston's apparently off-the-cuff video message after his meeting with Donald Trump twice referred to a 'strong' America. Strength is a quality which evangelical Christians have consistently said they admire in Trump.

Houston is well known and well networked among US evangelical prosperity preachers, who advocate loudly for the return of the strong white male in the face of creeping socialism and a feared weakening of sexual identity. And his network is ultimately a small world of big-name preachers who work with each other.

At the top of the pile, from Houston's earliest days in the pastoring business, is the veteran US pastor Tommy Barnett, a man Houston has hailed as 'my pastor'. Barnett began his ministry at the age of sixteen, improbable as that may seem. Now in his mid-80s, he is the chancellor of Southeastern University in Florida, a private school which is the largest Assemblies of God education facility in the United States. Barnett has become the face of a conservative Christian movement that is determined to restore the idea of the strong male to US society, based on Biblical principles. The movement is rooted in the belief that America has been weakened by decades of government policy that has supposedly eroded male identity.

Barnett is an adviser to an organisation called Promise Keepers, which is at the forefront of the move to restore the strong male and fight back against the advance of secular humanism.

This, the organisation claims, can only be achieved when men of integrity—'Promise-Keeping Men'—fulfil their destinies as godly husbands, fathers and leaders.

According to the organisation's mantra, a Promise Keeper is committed to practising spiritual, moral, ethical and sexual purity, and to building strong marriages and families through love, protection and Biblical values. A Promise Keeper is also committed to influencing his world by being obedient to the Great Commandment and the Great Commission, to 'go and make disciples of all nations, baptizing them in the name of the Father and of the Son and of the Holy Spirit'.

It is a measure of how connected Houston became in the United States that five US senators, all Republicans, presented themselves on a Sunday morning in August 2019 to the Hillsong complex in the Hills District of Sydney, a good 30 minutes' drive from the CBD.

The senators arrived as an official entourage, accompanied by their wives and officials, for a Sunday-morning service. According to US Senate records, they were part of an official delegation visiting Australia, New Zealand and Japan. Canberra was also on the itinerary.

The senators who made the trek to the House of Houston that morning were John Thune of South Dakota, James Lankford of Oklahoma, Richard Burr of North Carolina, Jerry Moran of Kansas and Tim Scott of South Carolina—all staunch religious conservatives and powerful operators in Republican Washington.

Richard Burr was the chair of the Senate Intelligence Committee when it investigated claims of Russian interference in the 2016 presidential election, and was a national security adviser to the Trump campaign.

John Thune was Senate majority whip and deputy to Mitch McConnell, who was then the Majority Leader. Senator Thune believes in creationism and had been involved in The Fellowship.

Jerry Moran was a former chair of the National Republican Senatorial Committee and chair of the Senate Veterans' Affairs Committee. Moran had lived for a period with other congressmen in The Fellowship's house in Washington. He was later found to be in breach of ethics rules by accepting the below-market rental rates offered to politicians. He described complaints about the arrangement as being rooted in 'a national effort to exclude matters of faith by public servants'.

James Lankford was co-chair of the bipartisan Congressional Prayer Caucus. Lankford was also a member of the advisory board of the Promise Keepers.

Tim Scott was the first African-American senator from the southern states of America since the Reconstruction era, a rising star who was elected with the backing of conservative Tea Party supporters. He would later nominate as a Republican candidate for the 2024 US presidential election.

All of them had made the journey to have a look-see at the place that was home to Hillsong's famous evangelical music, and that great Australian pastor Brian Houston.

Emperor Brian

By the start of 2020, global pastor Brian Houston was seemingly everywhere.

He practised what he had preached. Literally. Houston's vision of spreading his influence in the seven key sectors of society might well have reached its high point as he stood in President Trump's office, among the shiniest Pentecostal stars in the United States—influencing the most influential figure in the United States, the country of the great Pentecostal revival of the early 1900s.

Houston could boast of Hillsong Churches from coast to coast across the United States. Hillsong-branded churches were in Europe, the United Kingdom and Africa, on top of its Australian churches. Internal Hillsong records show such churches need to 'donate' 5 per cent of their total annual tithe income to 'Hillsong Global'.

There were a further 30 churches dotted around the world, all part of the so-called 'Hillsong Family', a form of partnership agreement between local churches and the transnational juggernaut. These were in Norway, Peru, Canada, Bulgaria, Columbia, Brazil, New Zealand, Indonesia, Mexico, Sweden, India and the Netherlands, as well as several in the United States and the United Kingdom.

Hillsong records show that these churches donate 3 per cent of their total annual tithes as 'membership' fees to Hillsong each year. In return, they can call themselves Hillsong Family Churches and attend the exclusive Hillsong Family Gathering twice a year at an overseas location.

Under an agreement offered by Hillsong HQ, there would be a 'relationship-based' arrangement with the 'Family Church', which would be a 'blessing to both parties as we focus on working towards the greater cause of Jesus Christ and building his church'. A Family Church would be entitled to use Hillsong branding 'up to the same size as your church's logo'; the Hillsong logo could be placed 'to the right of your church's logo'.

Hillsong had also added other, smaller churches to its growing network by taking them over.

Hillsong made its first move into Queensland in 2009 via an amalgamation with Garden City Christian Church in Brisbane, along with its regular attendees, who numbered some 4000 people. The amalgamation was done through a vote of the church's 900 or so 'members'—a different class to attendees, who have no voting rights. A 75 per cent majority of the vote was required to alter the church's financial arrangements. The Houstons won with 79 per cent of the vote. With it came, eventually, control over buildings and eight acres of land valued at some $8 million at the time.

The amalgamation infuriated some regular Garden City churchgoers. One complained that their church had 'totally lost its identity'.

'Without a moment to breathe, the leadership from Sydney suddenly arrived putting their stamp on this new way to "do church",' wrote former member Lance Goodall. 'We were presented with a spokesman for this, and a spokesman for that. We even had a special "money preacher" to encourage and remind us of the need to tithe and give generously.'

The incoming Houstons reportedly issued a statement to quell anger and offer assurances that church members would not lose control of their assets, although corporate records later showed that the church's registered office had moved to Hillsong HQ in Sydney, with all directors being from Hillsong.

This pattern would be repeated, more or less, in Melbourne and Perth, where former office holders of the smaller churches picked up roles with Hillsong. Hillsong pastors who had been with Brian Houston from the early days were now in charge in London and Johannesburg. Joel Houston was running New York. His brother, Ben, was running Los Angeles. Graduates of Hillsong College, established in the 1990s with two Sydney campuses offering courses to young Pentecostal Christians from around the world, were at work in New York and Dallas.

One of Hillsong's most influential former pastors, Michael Murphy, had 'planted' the Horizon Church, in Sydney's southern suburbs, which Scott Morrison had regularly attended before he became prime minister. Murphy had then moved on to head the Pentecostal training college in Parramatta, Alphacrucis University College, which struck teaching agreements with Hillsong. Murphy established a pastoring leadership consultancy, no doubt informed by his many years in Brian Houston's orbit.

On the Central Coast of New South Wales, the acclaimed Hillsong composer and singer Darlene Zschech, with her husband, Mark, built a network of Hillsong-style churches up and down the coast, as well as some in the United States and India.

A former Hillsong star named Christine Caine founded a non-profit organisation called the A21 Campaign to combat human trafficking. Caine had also established her own brand in the self-help and inspiration industry as a speaker and the author of some twenty books.

Hillsong College had become a magnet for young Christians working in the creative arts. They travelled to Sydney from around the world to learn the craft of worship music, film production, editing and graphics. Where else could a 22-year-old hope to work on a video that would garner a guaranteed million views? This had turned Hillsong into a kind of Hollywood for ambitious young Christians, where they would ply their trade—for little or no pay, if needed—in order to be noticed and promoted. And from Sydney they rebounded back into the world, to populate Hillsong's global enterprises and take its music even further afield.

Bobbie Houston, meanwhile, had built her own brand for Hillsong women, called the Colour Sisterhood, a global women's gathering, hosted in Sydney, London, Cape Town, New York, Los Angeles and Kiev.

Hillsong was a truly global operation. Brian Houston now held the title 'Global Senior Pastor', much as multinational conglomerates have a global CEO.

———

In Australia, Reverend Professor Philip Hughes, a researcher with the Christian Research Association, has charted what he calls the 'huge growth' in Pentecostalism, starting in the 1970s.

Between 1976 and 1981, according to the Australian census, the growth of Pentecostal worshippers in Australia was 88 per cent—a near doubling in numbers. Hughes found that Pentecostalism also grew strongly in the 1980s, with a doubling of numbers again between 1981 and 1991, at a time when most other Christian denominations were experiencing decline.

The rate of growth slowed in the 1990s, yet it was still just under 30 per cent for the decade. Between 2001 and 2011, there was a 22 per cent growth.

Then, for the first time, there was a fall. In the five years between 2016 and 2021, the census recorded a decline of 2 per cent, with the numbers of declared Pentecostals in Australia falling by nearly 5000.

Brian Houston was by far the most visible face of the nearly five decades of Hillsong growth, and he had been its most powerful driver as it had expanded from Sydney to the world and created its overwhelming online presence. He had always maintained his ability to speak fluent Jesus, but more and more over the years he had also adopted the mannerisms of corporate leadership. He was finely attuned to what the market wanted. And as the years went by, the market wanted less Genesis and Ephesians, and more about success and positivity. Accordingly, Houston morphed his religious talk into leadership talk, in line with the emerging cult of the corporate CEO as a superior being with special powers.

You could take your pick as to which of Brian's books you might read for self-help. All featured the ever-smiling face of the pastor, a picture of relaxed wealth. In 2015 he published *Live, Love, Lead*. In 2018 it was *There Is More: When the World Says You Can't, God Says You Can*.

The Hillsong brand was taking over the world—and what was Hillsong if not Brian Houston? The names were now virtually interchangeable. After 30 or more years, Brian Houston's brand was as big as, if not bigger than, that of the church he had created. Hillsong was Houston, and Houston was Hillsong. It was a concentration of fame and power not possible in the traditional Christian denominations, where the organisation is vastly bigger than the individual.

Organisationally, Houston had assumed all power within the church and its myriad companies and charities. In nearly all its corporate entities, the global senior pastor was the one and only director who was compulsorily appointed. Without the global senior pastor, the church's boards could not legally operate. This corporate structure meant nothing happened without Houston's approval. He had the power to appoint and remove pastors, which only created a cult of personal dependence and gratitude throughout the Hillsong empire.

In 2018, Houston had quietly taken a step that gave him power without limits. He removed Hillsong from the Australian Christian Churches (ACC) network, the umbrella organisation for Australia's thousand or more Pentecostal churches. Houston had previously been the ACC's national president for more than a decade, while other senior Hillsong figures had occupied board positions.

The separation meant that Hillsong was no longer subject to the governance and disciplinary processes of the ACC. It also meant Hillsong could use its own procedures to appoint and ordain pastors, and not be subject to the ACC's standards. Already Hillsong was arguably barely recognisable as a Pentecostal church, but now it was genuinely independent—and so was Brian Houston.

———

In a way, Brian Houston and Donald Trump were not such odd bedfellows after all. Both were opposed to the idea of government. Both were disdainful of secular accountability. Both praised the accumulation of wealth, and indeed revelled in it. Politically, both grafted themselves onto the US Republican Party, apparently simply because the party stood for small government and would back all religious demands.

Like Trump, Houston craved power, celebrity and fame. He surrounded himself with it, once he was ensconced in New York. Hillsong had always understood the power of celebrity endorsement. Now it boasted the star power of pop singer Justin Bieber, who had found his way in life again due to the efforts of Pastor Carl Lentz. The Bieber–Lentz relationship also made a celebrity of the young pastor, which in turn brought in more celebrities.

On every measure, Brian Houston appeared to break the old understandings of how Jesus wanted the world to be. Humble? Sitting with the poor? Shying away from the powerful and the wealthy? Not at Hillsong.

In his public appearances and on the preaching stage, Houston had always been an amiable presence. Here and there, in the midst of a passionate sermon on the Lord's power, he was capable of making the occasional self-deprecating comment. However, those close to him had also seen a streak of anger in him.

Years earlier, Hillsong's first music pastor, Geoff Bullock, had observed the two sides of Brian Houston. 'There was something lovable about Brian,' he said, 'and I think you'll find that still as a characteristic when people want to defend him, that he draws people's sympathy, and empathy.' At the same time, Bullock recalled, Houston had 'a pretty wild temper'. On some occasions Houston was known to go off over small details that hadn't been attended to.

In 2019 the darker side of Hillsong's global senior pastor was becoming more evident to those around him. Brian Houston was sitting on top of the world. And yet something seemed to have been eating him for almost a decade, and it was getting worse.

What on earth could that be?

5
REVELATIONS 1

The Sins of the Father

When Frank Houston washed ashore in Australia in the 1970s, he was an illustrious figure who had pioneered the growth of Pentecostalism in New Zealand's Assemblies of God churches. And it turned out that the Pentecostal church was the perfect place to be for Frank Houston. Much more so than the Baptist church, with its staid ways and traditional structure, where the local church reported upwards to regional and national bodies.

Frank Houston had created a church in which he could do pretty much as he pleased.

Between 1965 and 1977, Frank was the general super-intendent of the New Zealand Assemblies of God movement. As mentioned earlier, he spent weeks at a time away from his home and family as he moved around the country. Staying in contact was of course more difficult in those long-ago days, and Frank was able to live a separate life, well away from his wife, Hazel, and their children, Judith, Beverly, Brian, Graeme and Maureen.

Frank Houston's separate life was an extraordinary deception, but a deception not unknown in religious settings. Like most men of religion, he was a revered character in his community. Just as Catholic families were honoured to receive a priest into their homes, so it was with the anointed one, Frank Houston.

At the same time, his godly mission of saving souls gave him access to the vulnerable, including to children from broken homes.

———

One teenage boy was witness to both the public Frank Houston and the private, secret Frank Houston.

Peter Fowler was only fourteen years old when he caught the eye of the revered general superintendent, then aged 50 and at the peak of his influence in New Zealand's Pentecostal movement. Fowler was almost exactly the same age as Frank's elder son, Brian.

Fowler remembers travelling with Frank Houston to a church gathering at Whanganui, on the west coast of New Zealand, 200 kilometres north of Wellington. He watched as the great man was given a welcome fit for a prophet.

Frank Houston was larger than life. Good fun, occasionally tough, well known and well connected. All of which made the teenage Peter Fowler swell with pride when the country's leading Pentecostal figure said he would take him under his wing and make him a pastor.

Looking back, Fowler recognises that he was disconnected from his own family, vulnerable and subconsciously looking for a father figure. It was Frank who taught Peter how to do a perfect Windsor knot in his tie and took the boy along with him as he drove around New Zealand.

Peter Fowler didn't see what was coming next, but he certainly hasn't forgotten it.

'When he took me to Whanganui, we stayed in what I think was his sister's house,' he recalls. 'I mean, I got confused. Originally, I thought it was his mother. But in hindsight, I think it was his sister. And it was the house that they grew up in, and the mother had died.

'We were staying with his sister and were in a room, sharing a bed, a double bed. So he thought nothing about bringing this young guy from Wellington to share a bed in his sister's house. And I find it difficult to believe now that they didn't have some suspicions or some concerns.'

Houston, relying on the respect accorded to him as a man said to have been touched by the Holy Spirit, got away with it. And it would later emerge that he had very brazenly conducted a double life for decades.

'Interestingly, he never sought to meet my parents, and now we know why,' Fowler recalls.

The young Peter Fowler had already had a sexual encounter with a teenage girl before the pastor set his sights on him. He considers that the earlier experience had confirmed his sexuality to him, and he thus avoided what might have been a full identity breakdown. The trauma of that experience would later have an impact on Fowler in life-altering ways.

———

David Cowdrey was only eight years old when Frank Houston stole into his room and sexually abused him. Speaking 60 years later, Cowdrey well remembers how Houston manipulated events so as to enter the young boy's room while the adults in the house sat just down the hallway.

David's father was an elder at Frank Houston's church in Lower Hutt. On Saturday nights, the then 40-year-old pastor would arrive for Bible study and a prayer meeting in the lounge room of the family home in Tawa, a suburb of Wellington.

'Frank would visit my room on the excuse of going to the toilet,' David recalls. 'This black shadow would come into my room.'

For years, Cowdrey thought he was the only one who suffered in this way. He wasn't. Elsewhere in New Zealand, Frank Houston was using near-identical means to abuse other boys. Cowdrey later learnt that six others had been violated by Houston after he had been welcomed into the homes of church members who trusted him and were honoured to have him at their dinner table.

Being sexually abused by a man who claimed a direct relationship with the Holy Spirit provided an added layer of torment for boys raised as believers. David Cowdrey says he had a pattern of forever fighting with his bosses and the authority figures in his life. Peter Fowler says the betrayal set off a sequence of 'destabilising emotional events', which cut across his work life and his intimate relationships as an adult

The full, devastating effect of Frank Houston's crimes against boys took close to 25 years to emerge, but when it did, it set in train a series of events that would ultimately engulf Frank's own son, Brian.

Latter Rain of Shame

Brett Sengstock was a little boy in shorts, just seven years of age in 1970, when Frank Houston came to stay at the family home, right near the sun and surf of Coogee Beach, in Sydney's east.

Sengstock's family were pious people, heavily involved in the Assemblies of God movement. They were personal friends of the Houstons and were honoured to host the great New Zealand pastor, who was making more and more trips to Sydney as he prepared to establish a new frontier for his Latter Rain revivalist movement.

Frank Houston was then in his late forties. Occasionally he was joined by Hazel and Brian, who was undertaking Bible studies back home.

When the Houstons came to visit, the sleeping arrangements at the Sengstocks' Coogee home changed, and little Brett would sleep alone in a sectioned-off area on the verandah. It was there, one night in January 1970, that the abuse began.

Brett Sengstock made a record years later of what occurred:

Pastor Frank Houston would creep into my room late at night nearly every night of the week. I would be asleep when he came in and then I would wake up with him standing over me. I remember that when he was touching me inappropriately I would be petrified and would just lay very still. I could not speak while this was happening and felt like I could not breathe. I'm not sure how long he would stay in the room with me but it felt like forever. I know that he left when it was still full dark.

The abuse included Frank Houston lying on top of the little boy, inserting his finger into the boy's anus and also masturbating him.

Decades later, Brett Sengstock was able to recall the date of that first dead-of-night attack with clarity, because Houston had that day signed and dated his mother's Bible. The first day of the abuse was significant for another reason, too: it was the day before Brett's birthday.

The episode was the first of many. Brett Sengstock later spoke of the abuse continuing at his home as Frank Houston made more visits, with or without Hazel and Brian. Brett was also abused at different church meetings over a period of years. The Sengstock family followed Houston from church to church. They would see him before or after the meeting, and Houston would hug and kiss their son in front of others.

Brett recalled that the revered pastor would beckon him into his office, where he would run his hand between the boy's legs. It happened, too, at an Assemblies of God camp held at Windsor, at the time a rural town in the north-west of Sydney, which had been selected as a getaway place for the children of Assemblies of God families because of its remoteness away from the hustle and bustle of the city.

Many years later, at a royal commission, Sengstock would recall that Frank Houston's pursuit of him only stopped when he reached puberty—at which point, he said, 'Pastor Frank wanted nothing to do with me.'

Exactly when the abuse stopped—was the boy twelve or thirteen years old?—would later become a perverse focus for Hillsong's lawyers many years later. They wanted to make it clear that Frank Houston had committed the abuse when he was a visiting pastor from New Zealand, and therefore that the Hillsong Church bore no legal responsibility for his crimes.

———

Brett Sengstock was sixteen years old when he first raised the alarm. In 1978, he told his mother, who was still deeply involved with the church, as he set out in an official statement:

> I observed that it was difficult for her to accept what I told her. All of her friends were involved in the church, and the Houstons were considered to be almost like royalty in those circles. Pastor Frank was a very popular character and everyone wanted to go to his church in those days. After I told her about the abuse, my mother said words to the effect of: 'You don't want to be responsible for turning people from the church and sending them to hell.'
>
> My mother's response affected me and made me think that I did not want to cause any trouble. I therefore did not pursue the matter any further.

Sengstock was already carrying deep shame about the abuse when he finally told his mother. He carried that shame for decades more, along with a profound sense of rejection.

He described himself as feeling dead inside during this time. The abuse he suffered had destroyed his childhood.

For years, he said, he was 'full of shame, fear and embarrassment'. He dropped out of school in Year 10, aged sixteen. The abuse and the rejection had set him on a destructive course. He had a patchy work history. He was angry. He suffered from depression and was diagnosed with post-traumatic stress disorder. Years later, he continued to have flashbacks of Frank Houston in his bedroom. He had difficulty in his physical and emotional relationships with his wife and children.

After Brett's mother told him that he was causing trouble, it took a further twenty years before he once again confronted the abuse he had suffered. It wasn't his idea to do so. In fact, he had just wanted it all to go away.

It was the late 1990s, and the Houston family was mightier than ever. Together, Frank and Brian had risen to the summit of Australian Pentecostalism. Frank's church in central Sydney was always packed to overflowing. Out in the north-western suburbs, Brian's church was well on its way to becoming an international phenomenon. Hillsong's music had created a fever for Pentecostalism.

Brian wore the snazzy ties and jackets of the US pastors he admired. And more than that: he was the national president of the Assemblies of God network in Australia, the organisation that represented more than a thousand churches across the country.

It was amid this heady mix of power, money and fame that Brett Sengstock's case emerged. How it was handled by the

Houstons and their acolytes cast a deep shadow over Hillsong for decades. It also revealed a great deal about how the Houstons and the wider Pentecostal movement dealt with questions of accountability and the role of secular authorities.

Indeed, 1999 was the first time the Houstons were forced to confront a reputational crisis. It proved a defining moment, though.

A Grubby Deal on a McDonald's Napkin

Twenty years after hearing her son's story of abuse—and rejecting it—Brett Sengstock's mother told two Assemblies of God pastors what had happened to her son.

The secret was now out. Brett hadn't wanted it this way, and he was furious when he discovered what had happened. The Houstons were now involved. Their family friend Nabi Saleh, an 'elder' of the Hillsong Church and a multimillionaire businessman, would play a pivotal role in dealing with what became known as 'the Sengstock issue'.

Brett Sengstock's case was the thread that, when pulled, unravelled Frank Houston's secret and decades-long life as a paedophile—and, sinfully for the church, a man with homosexual desires. But Sengstock's revelations were, as far as is known, the first time Frank Houston was forced to confront this ugly truth.

When told of the allegation, Frank Houston contacted Brett Sengstock's mother and Brett himself. Houston said he was calling to apologise. But Brett didn't see it that way. To his mind, Houston had two aims: to keep a lid on the information and to have Brett Sengstock forgive him, so that he could die with a clear conscience. The pastor was then 77 years of age and still had several years to live.

Frank Houston came up with a plan. He would pay Brett Sengstock some money. The initial amount would be $2000. The plan though fell through.

After some to-ing and fro-ing, Frank Houston arranged a meeting that would settle things once and for all. Houston, the biggest name in Australian Pentecostalism, would meet with this boy from his past, who was now a badly damaged 36-year-old man suffering the full emotional and physical legacy of profound childhood trauma.

According to later royal commission evidence by Sengstock, Houston arranged for the meeting to take place at a McDonald's outlet in Sydney's northern suburbs, well away from his inner-city church. Sengstock arrived alone. Houston was accompanied by his close friend Nabi Saleh, who drove them in his green Jaguar. Brian later described Saleh's role as providing support for his father. 'Nabi Saleh was a family friend,' Brian Houston later said. 'He loved my dad and I think he just—all he was concerned about was looking after my father in terms of driving him there and being there to comfort him. Obviously, you know, for my father, it was probably a—you know, a difficult day, and he was just there literally to stand with him.'

Either way Saleh's presence meant Sengstock was out-numbered and outgunned.

The men sat down and Saleh began eating a burger. The deal was that Brett Sengstock would be paid $10,000 and in return he would forgive Frank. End of story. Brett Sengstock signed on a dirty McDonald's paper napkin—the same napkin, it turned out, that Saleh had used while eating his burger.

There it was. Done and dusted. Talk about cheap at twice the price. If the Sengstock case had been settled in court, the compensation due to him for pain, suffering, health and lost earnings might have run into the hundreds of thousands of dollars. The Catholic Church under George Pell was offering victims of abuse by its clergymen $50,000 in compensation at this time, as well as some form of counselling, under its 'Melbourne Response' protocol.

Even then, the Houstons had to be prodded into actually paying the money. When nothing had arrived in the weeks after the deal was done, Sengstock spoke with Brian Houston. Subsequently, a cheque for $10,000 arrived in the mail. There was no note attached, though a magistrate later ruled that it wasn't hush money.

Doing a dirty deal, dirt cheap and in secret, was to become a trademark Houston way of settling grievances.

———

So much for the money. But there was also the question of Frank Houston's reputation within Australian Pentecostalism as the man who had paved the way for the giant Hillsong Church, to say nothing of his future as a pastor in his own inner-Sydney church. The responsibility for all that fell to the person who was the worst placed to handle it: Frank's own son Brian.

Brian Houston had a profound conflict of interest. He was the head of the Assemblies of God Australia, the very body that would need to investigate the allegation made against Frank Houston, and that would have to decide on a course of action if the claim were found to be credible. That action might mean anything from removing Frank from duty to reporting him to the police.

Brian Houston found out about the claim of sexual abuse against Brett Sengstock in a meeting with Hillsong's general manager, George Aghajanian, in October 1999. Aghajanian had been contacted with word from the field by a Sydney-based pastor.

Brian Houston has spoken many times about the moment he found out that his father had sexually abused a child, and its impact on him. Here was a 45-year-old man learning the grim truth about his father, who was also his hero and mentor. His most candid account of this was given at a very public hearing in 2014, where it was televised and viewed, ultimately, by millions of people.

The Royal Commission into Institutional Responses to Child Sexual Abuse was a five-year-long inquiry set up by the government of Julia Gillard in January 2012. The chief commissioner was Peter McClellan, a retired New South Wales judge, and it is generally referred to as the McClellan Inquiry.

In October 2014 Brian Houston appeared before the commission. He recalled in his testimony that, one day, at the conclusion of a church meeting, his general manager George Aghajanian had told him that he needed to speak to him about his father.

'I could tell by his face that this was not going to be good, and my stomach dropped,' Brian Houston testified. 'And then he just went on and proceeded to tell me what's in the documentation, and that is that someone had rung just one of the pastors in our church and started to, basically, just blurt out all this stuff about Frank, my dad.

'But it was very clear that he was talking about a minor. The reason I remember is because it hit me, you know, in a ten-second period, in a wave, because I was, like, "homosexual", you know, get my head around that, before my consciousness went to, "Hold on a minute, we're not just talking about, you know, homosexual; we're talking about paedophilia." So I can still remember it very clearly.

'[After that I] cried. Went home and I was devastated, to be honest with you. I was totally devastated. My father was away. I'm pretty sure he was going to be away for another three weeks, and so I determined that once he got back, I had no choice, absolutely no choice, but to confront him. It was something that I completely dreaded having to do.

'I knew deep down in my stomach. Somehow deep down in my stomach, I knew. I can't say why, but I feel like I didn't doubt the truth of [the statements].

'I felt—I felt that this is not a good situation, that, you know, it's not going to have a good ending.

'I can't say I wasn't entirely surprised—I was totally shocked and traumatised. It's just that somehow, call it instinct, I had a feeling that this is not just a malicious [rumour]—you know.

'It's humiliating to me today that I have to walk out there to cameras, and so on, about the fact that my father is a known serial paedophile, yes.'

———

The question of what Brian Houston did with the information he had received about his father in 1999 followed him for more than two decades until he was acquitted at trial for any criminal liability for failing to disclose it. Brian Houston always maintained that he handled the complexity of these relationships properly.

Frank Houston was soon told he could no longer preach. Brian took over Frank's role as senior pastor at his central-Sydney church, while also running his own church, soon to be renamed Hillsong, in the Hills District.

Brian called an emergency meeting of the Assemblies of God's national executive to work out a solution to the Frank Houston problem. As national president, he would normally have chaired the meeting. On this occasion he stood aside, but he stayed in the room—a decision for which he was later criticised by the McClellan Inquiry.

That meeting is remarkable in many respects.

First, it was decided that the minutes of the meeting would be kept confidential and held in a special file. It was also resolved that, 'in the interest of the complainant', the Assemblies of God movement would not be notified of disciplinary action against Frank Houston. Most strikingly, the allegation made against Frank Houston was noted in the minutes as an allegation 'of a single act of sexual abuse more than 30 years ago'. The Assemblies of God's official record therefore seriously understated Frank Houston's crimes.

Brian Houston later said it was the most he could get his father to acknowledge. But that statement in itself only makes clear that someone independent was needed if the truth were to be uncovered.

The meeting noted that 'the complainant [did] not wish to be identified and [did] not wish to make a formal complaint', and that the executive had taken legal advice on its obligations. The victim's reluctance to take action would later become Brian Houston's primary defence for not having informed the police of Frank Houston's sexual abuse of a child.

Brian Houston also later asserted that Brett Sengstock was in a 'brittle state' at the time and that, as a 36 year old, he was an adult, he was able to make his own decision as to whether to go to the police or not.

This was controversial and dangerous territory for Brian Houston, who later said he had no doubt that his father, then 77 years of age, would have gone to prison for his crimes.

Brett Sengstock later explained how he was thinking at the time. A supportive pastor had told him that she believed him, but that 'the secular courts is [sic] not the way . . . to go'. She advised him to go through Assemblies of God church processes, which, she believed, would mean he would receive 'a fair hearing'. He said it had never occurred to him to go to the police or the courts.

'Well, "the secular courts", as I understood it then, was the courts of the earth,' he said later. 'Being so heavily involved in the church, we looked to the church for direction, and that's the way we seemed to be programmed to deal with these problems. So we went to the church. The secular courts and the police were something that was for the unbelievers.'

Decades later, in 2023, a Sydney court accepted that Brian Houston had a reasonable excuse for not reporting the Sengstock case to the authorities and acquitted him of the criminal charge of concealment.

'We're a Compassionate Church, I Feel'

The Brett Sengstock case was a turning point for the Houston family given their stature within the Pentecostal movement. Quietly, word spread within the movement of Frank Houston's 'moral failure', as it was styled.

A one-off? Thirty years ago? That was how Frank Houston preferred to have everyone think of it, with little or no detail being aired. Luckily for him, the Houstons' acolytes in the senior ranks of the Australian Pentecostal movement were prepared to go along with this characterisation of events.

The truth was quite different. The Sengstock case had flushed out stories of abuse by Frank Houston from across the Tasman—though only a handful of senior figures clustered around the family were in the know.

When the Australian Assemblies of God leadership met their New Zealand counterparts in 2000, they learnt of widespread rumours among New Zealand's pastors. They were told that rumours had been circulating for at least three years in relation to Frank Houston having 'improper dealings' with young boys more than 30 years earlier. At least 50 pastors in New Zealand were aware of these allegations. This included a group of 30 who had been discussing the matter on a recent boat trip.

For nearly all of that period, New Zealand's pastors had held the line when it came to secrecy.

Six specific allegations were eventually investigated by the New Zealand executive relating to improper touching of genitals. The New Zealand executive believed the allegations were 'substantial' and accepted that they had no reason to doubt them.

All the complainants wanted was for justice to be done, the Australian Pentecostal leaders were told. Yet that was the last thing they were going to receive.

Two New Zealand victims, David Cowdrey and Peter Fowler, made approaches to the Houstons and sought to have them at least acknowledge the misdeeds of Frank's past. It's worth dwelling on how the Houstons dealt with these complaints because they, along with Brett Sengstock, set the template for the years to come.

In short, those who arrived with a grievance were treated as a nuisance. The Houston family had known Peter Fowler and David Cowdrey in New Zealand. David Cowdrey's father, Maurice, had sat on the board of Frank Houston's church in Lower Hutt, and had helped guide its growth. But that wasn't worth a jot when the crunch came.

Peter Fowler, who was fourteen when he was abused by Frank Houston, had moved to Sydney by the early 2000s when the truth was starting to emerge. Fowler was then in his mid-forties. The New Zealand Assemblies of God made inquiries on his behalf in 2003.

As he tells it: 'I was open to forgiveness, really. But the word was that Frank was not well enough, that he had Alzheimer's and wouldn't know who I was. They said he was too far gone to be able to meet with him. Now, that was a lie because we know that he was well enough to do other things, including even preaching in a church that Brian allowed at the time. So they were absolutely protecting him and preventing any kind of meeting with me, any kind of reconciliation.'

Frank Houston's crimes against Peter Fowler had been committed in New Zealand. So Hillsong—an Australian entity, and one that had not even existed at the time the offences occurred—had no legal obligations towards Fowler. But what of the moral case? After all, Brian Houston and Hillsong were the successors to Frank Houston and his pioneering church movements in New Zealand and Sydney. And it was a church, after all.

Fowler knew it was too late for a criminal prosecution of Frank Houston, and he had little expectation that the Houstons would come up with any reasonable compensation unless they absolutely had to. In any case, he was seeking other things: a meeting with Frank Houston (or his representatives), an acknowledgement that the offence had taken place and, finally, an apology—none of which would cost a cent.

Fowler's case was raised years later with Brian Houston during the McClellan Inquiry. At the royal commission, Houston was resolute on one point: he bore no responsibility for the actions of his father.

'I was aware of [Peter Fowler's] complaint,' Houston told the inquiry, 'and the executive agreed that this was a New Zealand issue. It happened in New Zealand before Frank ever pastored in Australia. My feeling, really, was that it was all about vindication and compensation.'

Houston said he was aware that Frank Houston's victim was living in Australia, but was quick to add that 'when this happened in New Zealand, I was a teenager [and] Hillsong Church didn't exist'.

This was a common refrain at the royal commission. In the case of another unnamed teenage victim, Brian Houston accepted that the boy had been grievously damaged, but when it came to what the victim wanted—which included a chance to speak to all the pastors at Hillsong Church about abuse— he too was to be 'pointed towards' New Zealand.

'When these things happened, Hillsong didn't exist,' Houston proffered again. 'We're a compassionate church, I feel, and, to be honest, what he was asking for wasn't going to cost a bundle of money . . . I think more we just felt that . . . there's a New Zealand Assemblies of God; there is a New Zealand Lower Hutt Assemblies of God where my father was the pastor, and the best place for him to go and ask these questions was there.'

Ultimately, the Houstons were clear that what had happened to Peter Fowler wasn't their concern. Fowler was eventually paid compensation of NZ$25,000 by the New Zealand Assemblies of God after a brief investigation that corroborated details of his story. These included Fowler's memory of being taught how to tie a Windsor knot—a sure sign to those in the know that Frank Houston was involved. There was a further detail, too, which implicated Frank Houston: the abuse had arisen from the senior pastor's habit of play-fighting with young people.

There was another reason for the Houstons to ignore Peter Fowler—one that is directly related to the power struggle raging in Australian Pentecostalism and the Houstons' determination to squash any and all dissent. If the full truth about Frank Houston had emerged in the late 1990s and early 2000s, it would risk fatally wounding the entire Hillsong enterprise.

Peter Fowler's complaint about Frank Houston had been supported by an Australian pastor called Philip Powell—a man who had long campaigned against the Houstons' style of Pentecostalism, the money-go-round they had built and the all-entertainment pageantry they had made of religion.

Early in the piece—it's hard to know exactly when—Powell had been aware of child sex abuse allegations against Frank Houston in New Zealand, and had attempted to expose him within the Assemblies of God movement. This, of course, made Powell a prime threat to the Houstons' hold on Australian Pentecostalism.

In the witness box, Brian Houston explained that he hadn't met Peter Fowler personally because of the role played by someone he called a 'well-known mischief-maker' in the Australian Assemblies of God at the time. Houston told the inquiry that having this mischief-maker 'putting his weight behind this guy [Peter Fowler]' had made things 'very difficult'.

Brian Houston didn't name Philip Powell but insiders knew exactly who he was referring to.

———

Peter Fowler had hit a brick wall, and David Cowdrey didn't do much better.

Some 50 years later, in 2009, in the years before the royal commission began, David Cowdrey's wife, Denise, took up the cudgels on behalf of her broken husband to seek a form of justice for Frank Houston's abuse. Denise Cowdrey wrote to Brian Houston via the Hillsong contact form on the church's website. Frank Houston was no longer alive:

> Could you please contact me urgently about your father and my husband. David's mother is about to be 80 and I would really like all this abuse stuff sorted before she moves off to heaven. What your father did to my husband has had an impact on all our lives. To move forward we need to deal with it. Sorry, realise it wasn't you; but unfortunately I think you are the only one to deal with it.

Brian Houston responded that he was 'very alarmed and shocked' about what had happened. He also remembered David 'very well as a kid' and had 'often wondered what had happened to him'.

'Whereabouts in New Zealand do you live?' Houston asked. 'I will be in Auckland April/May and would be very happy to catch up with David.'

Cowdrey says he heard nothing more from Brian Houston after the email, and that he 'couldn't do it' anyway. 'I was too broken,' he says. As well as that, the Cowdrey budget didn't run to the cost of a flight from Nelson to Auckland. 'Financially I was in a bit of a mess too.'

Hillsong was bringing in tens of millions of dollars in tax-free income via tithes, donations and its stratospherically success-ful music. In legal terms, Brian Houston owed David Cowdrey nothing. But was there any offer to help out?

'No, there wasn't. There was nothing more than the email,' Cowdrey remembers. Not that he was looking for much: 'A phone call from Brian would have been healing.'

Royal commission evidence years later confirmed to David Cowdrey that he was not alone. To that extent it finally brought some clarity on the ordeal he had gone through as a little boy.

'When I read Brett Sengstock's testimony from the royal commission in 2014, it was identical to what I went through as an eight-year-old. It was my "a-ha!" moment about what had happened to me in 1962,' he says. 'I never had the language to explain it. So I talked about the "black shadow" coming into my room. That's how I explained it to my parents.' The lack of any gesture from Brian Houston to help the Cowdreys move forward disappointed David, but did not surprise him. His family and the Houstons went back decades. 'I grew up with Brian and [Brian's brother] Graeme. We were good friends,' he recalls.

Cowdrey contemplated taking legal action against Frank Houston's old church in Lower Hutt, but he was unable to muster support. He never received an apology from anyone.

Burying the Truth

When Frank Houston died in 2004, five years after the Sengstock allegations were dealt with by Australia's Pentecostal leaders, he received a hero's funeral. Whatever the great man's crimes, there was none that couldn't be overlooked for the occasion.

The funeral of the man hailed as the father of Australia's Pentecostal churches attracted a thousand mourners and dignitaries.

They included the deputy commissioner of the New South Wales Police Force, Andrew Scipione, a devout Christian who later rose to the rank of commissioner; federal parliamentarian Louise Markus, a member of Hillsong; and famous jockey Darren Beadman, who had been converted to the Christian ranks by the much-loved pastor.

Some newspapers carried the erroneous story that Houston— an otherwise good man—had committed a one-off sexual offence involving a boy in New Zealand 30 years before. Another time. Another country.

The *Sydney Morning Herald*'s report included the detail that Frank Houston had been sacked by his own son 'after he admitted having sexually abused a boy in New Zealand more than 30 years ago'.

This was patently wrong, but you couldn't blame the journalists. This false story had been given currency by Australia's Pentecostal church hierarchy. Brian Houston himself did nothing to dispel it. 'He was a man who perhaps made some big mistakes a long time ago,' Brian told mourners, 'but everyone here knows that he was a man who stood for what he believed in.'

When Frank Houston was seen off to meet his maker, the full truth about his misdeeds went with him. Brian Houston didn't let on, it seems, to the future New South Wales police commissioner standing in the midst of the mourners.

So what exactly was going on that day, as the grief-stricken gathered around the coffin of the great man?

It was, it seems, part of a confused public narrative lasting more than a decade which had the effect of distancing Hillsong from Frank Houston's sordid past—as the church thrust ever higher, faster and stronger, reeling in a fortune on its image as a modern, wholesome spiritual alternative.

At the heart of the confusion was the clear impression that Frank Houston had committed his crimes only in New Zealand and not in a little boy's room in Sydney, Australia, in a house barely thirty minutes' drive away from Frank's funeral.

In early 2003, well over a year before Frank Houston's death, Brian Houston gave his most extensive interview yet about his father. The report in the *Sydney Morning Herald* conveyed the inference that Frank Houston committed his abuse in New Zealand.

The newspaper reported that 'finding out his father had abused a child back in New Zealand' was 'like the jets flying into the twin towers of my soul'.

The *Sydney Morning Herald* reported that Houston had removed his father from all roles in the church but that he 'did not contact police in New Zealand' because the victim was old enough to do that himself.

In other respects, the *Sydney Morning Herald* account matched Houston's actions on the Sengstock issue. 'Basically I received a complaint, so I confronted my father and he admitted it,' Houston had said.

'I told our church what had happened [several months after he found out], but as soon as I found out I told the elders of this church and the Assemblies of God,' Houston says. 'To my congregation, when I told them, I used words like predator and sexual abuse and so on—I did not try to hide it.'

Yet in the *Sydney Morning Herald*, Brian Houston's reported remarks—that the crime occurred in New Zealand—placed the crime outside the jurisdiction of NSW authorities, at a time when Frank Houston was alive and potentially open to police investigation.

The report's author, veteran journalist, Greg Bearup, recalls that he wrote his account from tape recordings of interviews with Brian Houston. Bearup says there was never a request for a correction.

Brian Houston had earlier spoken of his father's abuse at a Hillsong sermon in 2002. Houston related that 'in late 1999, early 2000', he had learnt for the first time, from 'one of my staff coming and relaying a complaint', that his father had committed offences. This, he said, had happened 'while he was still a pastor in New Zealand thirty years ago or more'. The revelation had hit him with a force which he compared to 'jets flying into the Twin Towers', another reference to the 9/11 attacks carried out by al-Qaeda on New York's World Trade Center.

Given the timing, the reference was clearly to Sydney boy Brett Sengstock. Whether or not he intended it, Houston's formulation was ambiguous at best and misleading at worst.

The wider church movement had also bought the idea of the incident occurring in New Zealand. It was certainly more palatable—perhaps even more *forgivable*—than the true story, which was that, as well as abusing the teen-aged Fowler, Frank Houston had crept into the bedroom of the seven-year-old Brett Sengstock to sexually abuse him, night after night, in the family home at Coogee Beach, Sydney.

That truth only became known to the public during the hearings of the McClellan Inquiry in 2014. It came as a shock to the many Assemblies of God preachers in Australia who had not been privy to the secrets of the Houstons.

———

Years after his death, more accounts emerged on Frank Houston's homosexuality. In this case his actions had all been done under the guise of 'counselling' or gay conversion therapy.

Peter Laughton was 23 years old when he went to see Pastor Frank Houston around 1980 about his homosexuality. Houston was then in his late fifties.

'My counselling sessions by the senior minister were nothing more than sexual abuse disguised in the form of the need of a father's love and discipline,' Laughton later disclosed in a speech to an LGBTI network which aims to build bridges with religious organisations. 'Through my naivety, I enjoyed the naked beatings, the eternal bum caresses and masturbating into bottles, among other things.'

Laughton was training to be a pastor. Corporate documents show that he was a director of Houston's Sydney Christian Life Centre for almost two years in 1990, a position he held through the grace and favour of Frank.

He said the abuse continued for about four years. 'I was in total denial, believing that I was a whole delivered-and-on-fire-for-God heterosexual. I married and had three beautiful children and became a fiery AOG [Assemblies of God] preacher and pastor, and remained that way for twenty-three years.'

Laughton's marriage later broke down. The pretence that he was heterosexual was over.

Frank Houston not only sexually abused children as young as seven and had unfettered access to vulnerable children in New Zealand and Australia, as well as on several Pacific islands where he led Christian missionary work, he also had sexual relations with young-adult males under the guise of conducting gay conversion therapy as a senior pastor. All that time his church maintained that homosexuality was a sin. Frank's life of hypocrisy and deception was a high-wire act that depended on iron-clad systems to prevent the truth from emerging.

That, in combination with the shame felt by victims and a reluctance by believers to go to secular authorities, means that the true scale of Frank Houston's crimes is unknown.

Through his statements, Brian Houston knowingly or unknowingly created the view that his father's crimes against children were committed in New Zealand, with no mention of offending after he arrived in Australia.

The story of Sydney boy Brett Sengstock punctured the view that Houston had only abused children in New Zealand. But Brian Houston and Hillsong's lawyers were adamant that Houston was only visiting from New Zealand when he abused Sengstock from 1970. Their argument has been that whatever Frank had done had nothing to do with Hillsong or any of its predecessor organisations.

But the case of Darcy Johnson, never before told, shows that Frank Houston continued to offend against children after he established his church in Australia, under the aegis of the Australian Assemblies of God.

A Story Never Told

It has taken Darcy Johnson 40 years to tell his story.

Darcy Johnson is a name he is using to enable him to speak of his experiences while maintaining his privacy. Now in his late forties, he has built a new life away from the Pentecostal church and away from Australia. He has a young family and would prefer to get on with life without carrying the tag of being a victim of Frank Houston.

Yet Johnson is moved to tell his story, partly to help piece together the truth on Frank Houston and partly to show others abused by Houston in Australia that they are not alone.

'In the years since I left the church I have progressively come to terms with what happened through secular counselling, and with time I feel I am in a better place. Seeing recent documentaries on Hillsong opened up old memories, I even cried a little.

'However it did provide me with a sense of accountability, that someone else could see this, that someone else saw that what happened was wrong.'

Darcy Johnson's story begins in 1984. He was eight years of age.

By this stage Frank Houston had made a permanent move from New Zealand and had established his Sydney Christian Life Centre in 1977. He was the senior pastor and his church was affiliated with the Assemblies of God in Australia.

Darcy's father was an active member of Frank Houston's church in inner Sydney, attracted to the pastor's alluring message of Godly prosperity. Frank Houston was pleased to have a wealthy businessman in the flock.

Thus the conditions were laid down for young Darcy's abuse. Frank Houston, the accomplished predator, had a habit of abusing the trust vested in him by parents. When it came to the crunch, parents would always take the word of the great man of God over that of their own children.

Darcy's family were model parishioners, often attending two services on Sundays as they followed Frank Houston between churches, joining him for lunch and helping out with the cleaning.

It wasn't long before the young boy became part of Frank Houston's special group.

'Frank had a group of boys, about my age and a few years older,' Darcy recalls. 'He would refer to us as Frank's boys, his mighty young men of God. He would work with us directly, laying healing hands on us and have prophecies for us, known as "words", meaning God's word.

'Using his access to me, he would fondle and touch me inappropriately. He would justify this by saying he was anointed by the Holy Spirit and that it was key to my growth.

'This happened on a regular basis and for me was always on a one-to-one and in an isolated area. These activities would occur in the offices in Darlinghurst, or when we would find ourselves isolated within the church complex and at times when attending lunches or events between Sunday services.'

Darcy's memory is that the physical rituals of Pentecostalism were central to Houston's grooming of boys.

'I never saw anyone else publicly abused, but outwardly in front of the congregation he would pray over and lay hands on us,' Darcy says.

'This did extend to water baptism, where we would be made to stand in front of him, both of us in the water and then dunked back under water. This was done to gain trust and qualify his actions, which then created a position of trust with our parents, leading to one-on-one sessions where the abuse would occur.'

As Darcy grew a little older—around the age of twelve— Frank Houston invited him to prayer and healing and guidance sessions, which were always one on one, with the boy left feeling isolated.

'The sessions included groping and fondling and he would put my hand on him. There was never any penetration, or oral type of activity. I always managed to wriggle out of things and run away, maybe if I had not gotten away it could have escalated. I honestly got to the point where it was almost like a game, to get away from him, or to try and avoid him completely,' he says.

As Darcy showed signs of puberty, Frank Houston appeared to lose interest in him. Brett Sengstock had the same experience.

As Darcy Johnson moved further afield, as a young Pentecostal Christian he would discover that outside the Houston bubble others had their doubts about the great preacher and his special relationship with the boys of his church.

Darcy had joined the Royal Rangers, a Pentecostal outreach group for young people, similar to the scouts.

As part of the Rangers, Darcy would attend Ranger events where other 'outposts' would join.

'People would make the connection that our outpost was from Frank Houston's church and make jokes at our expense involving Frank Houston. They would ask about what they had heard of Frank's habit of touching boys.'

Darcy says that after he joined a new outpost in another part of Sydney his new leader informed him that things were done differently there.

'On one occasion he told me that what happened at my old outpost, the Sydney Christian Life Centre, did not happen here and that they protected children.

'He never specifically said anything about Frank but people didn't like to mention things. In general, the Assemblies of God group was very wary of the organisation being tarnished. There was also a process where things that happened in the church were one hundred per cent dealt with from within the church.

'We were brought up to believe that we were only account-able to Jesus, and we only had to ask him for forgiveness and our sins would be washed clean,' Darcy says.

As a teenager and a young adult Darcy says he tried 'many times' to tell his parents what Houston had done to him. He was told that God was the ultimate judge and that any issues should be addressed internally by church leadership. A Sunday school teacher he confided in had concluded that he was 'troubled' and that nothing further should be done.

'Overall, the church sold us a story about being close to, showing respect for and to honour God, Jesus, the Holy Spirit, church leadership and finally our parents. The church did everything it could to convince us that there was a correlation between financial success and our place in heaven. Our job was to help grow the church, and not to question it or in any way cause trouble,' he concluded.

Darcy Johnson's account is the first to show that there were suspicions within other Australian Pentecostal churches about Frank Houston's sordid behaviour with children stretching back to the 1980s.

It also explains exactly why no one did anything about it.

Darcy Johnson's story also makes clear why it was so hard for Brett Sengstock, even as a man in his late thirties, to go outside the bubble of the church and take his complaint about Frank Houston to the police. Sengstock's reluctance later became the reasonable justification—accepted by a court—for Brian Houston's decision not to inform police of his father's crimes.

6

REVELATIONS 2

The Sins of the Son

The night in July 2019 when Brian Houston brought Scott Morrison, the newly re-elected Prime Minister of Australia, up on stage to join him, to rapturous applause, was the opening night of that year's annual Hillsong Conference. It seemed at the time like a fabulously auspicious start, but at some point in that week of conferencing another Houston emerged.

At the end of one of those days, after the crowds had evaporated away, Houston gathered with other Hillsong luminaries for drinks at the five-star Pullman Hotel at Sydney Olympic Park. After one or perhaps a dozen drinks too many, Houston took the lift upstairs to the hotel's executive floor, reserved for VIP guests.

Emerging from the lift, he was apparently unable to find his room key. Rather than return to hotel reception, Houston went to the room of a woman who had also been at the hotel bar, and who was known to Houston as a financial supporter of the church.

Houston knocked on the door, went inside and remained in the woman's hotel room for a period said to be 40 minutes.

What happened in that Pullman Hotel room that night was kept secret for more than three years. It was later claimed that Houston had become disoriented by a cocktail of anxiety tablets and alcohol. This meant that he had no clear recollection of what he and his female companion had done. She, too, had no coherent recollection of what had occurred.

That's what Hillsong later claimed, anyway. The woman in question has never spoken publicly about the matter. Amid the confusion and the cover-up, one thing is certain: the tectonic plates of the life of Brian Houston had begun to shift.

Unbeknown to Hillsong's hundreds of thousands of followers, their prophet-pastor, the leader with the direct relationship with God, had been held together by booze and tablets for many years. Those in the inner circle knew that Houston had been a heavy drinker. A very small, tight-knit group also knew—but kept it to themselves—that Houston had flirted via text with a junior female staff member some years prior to the events of 2019. That young woman had left her work at Hillsong Church, distressed at the treatment she had received.

However, by 2019, the biggest secret of all had returned to haunt Houston. Police had begun to investigate the allegations that he had failed to tell the authorities what he knew of his father's paedophile crimes. These allegations stretched back all of twenty years. They had emerged and gone away again, because the trail to the past seemed too distant. Now, however, the police were back investigating the Houston family secret, and Brian had good reason to be on alert.

Houston's days at the top were numbered then. As it happened, so were Scott Morrison's.

————

Brian Houston's fall from the peak of Pentecostal power followed a familiar pattern. Some of the ministers of religion with whom the Houstons had been close had fallen from grace long before the global senior pastor began his precipitous descent.

Take, for example, David Yonggi Cho, who at one point had built his Yoido Full Gospel Church in South Korea to a congregation of 800,000. He had had a major impact on the growth of Pentecostalism in Australia and had appeared on stage with the Houstons in the early years as they barnstormed around the country. The prosperity gospel certainly worked for him.

But his glorious career ended up in inglorious controversy. In 2014 Cho was convicted of embezzling US$12 million of church funds, having directed his church's leaders to buy unlisted stock owned by his son. He was found guilty of tax evasion.

Cho declared his day of judgement as the harshest day of his life of ministry. 'All I did was offer my life just like the boy who gave the five loaves and two fish. I simply held on to the dreams that the Lord gave me,' the 78-year-old said in a statement. Cho was given a suspended sentence of three years and was fined nearly US$5 million.

Yonggi Cho's was an extraordinary decline, but it's hard to beat the American televangelists when it comes to the full techni-colour fall from grace.

Jim Bakker and Jimmy Swaggart, in particular, provided the template for the false-prophet American preacher. Both were liars and fraudsters whose time ended in tears amid public confessions about having been caught by the Devil.

Pentecostal televangelist Jim Bakker and his 'Praise the Lord' ministries raked in millions upon millions of dollars from his loyal and gullible followers via an imaginative venture called Heritage USA, a theme park which at one point was the third-most successful theme park in America. Bakker was a terrific television performer, a skill he honed over successive programs broadcast on Christian networks, including the Christian Broadcasting Network, which was owned by the conservative Christian busi-nessman and Republican Party figure Pat Robertson.

Quizzed on his prolific television output, Bakker famously responded: 'I believe if Jesus was alive today he would be on TV.'

Bakker and his wife, Tammy Faye, formed the perfect Christian union. They were wholesome, a bit hokey and wildly successful. That is, until it was revealed in 1987 that Jim had raped a young woman who was working as a church secretary, and then paid for her silence with hush money of over a quarter of a million dollars. The rape occurred in 1980 and had been kept under wraps for seven years. A separate investigation found that he had diverted US$4 million of church funds for his and Tammy Faye's personal use.

America's other infamous fallen preacher, Jimmy Swaggart also fell to Earth in the late 1980s. Swaggart's worldwide ministry had seen him team up with Frank Houston in the early days of the Assemblies of God movement in Australia.

As we saw earlier, Jimmy Swaggart's golden career began with his nationally networked television program, *Camp Meeting Hour*, which was eventually transmitted via 3000 stations and cable networks each week. Swaggart was the son of a fiddle-playing Pentecostal preacher, Willie Swaggart. At seventeen years of age, Jimmy married fifteen-year-old Frances Anderson, whom he met through church. The two lived in poverty as they moved around rural Louisiana, with Jimmy preaching from a flatbed trailer. He also had a great singing voice.

Swaggart's extraordinary rags-to-riches story ended in disgrace in 1988, when it emerged that he'd had sex with a prostitute. This led to his famous 'I have sinned' television confession, in which he tearfully apologised to his family, his congregation and the wider world.

Three years later Swaggart was pulled over by police and found with a sex worker who he had picked up from the side of the road. This time, Swaggart was not so effusive in his apologies. 'The Lord told me it's flat none of your business,' the pastor told his followers.

As later events would show, that was a line the Lord apparently gave to several church leaders, including a number at Hillsong.

———

Like his infamous predecessors, Brian Houston was wildly successful as a salesman for Jesus. Indeed, on paper, Pastor Brian was the living embodiment of the prosperity gospel he promoted, with the world outside a small inner circle having no clue that Brian too had committed his own moral transgressions and was living on the edge. Outwardly he and Bobbie were the image of a happy, loving couple. Their three children were thriving and sharing in the success of the family business. Brian had his late-model Audi and the Harley-Davidson for tooling around town.

The Houstons had their sprawling family home in the outer north-west of Sydney, which—along with the rest of the Sydney property market—grew in value day by day. Brian and Bobbie would occasionally repair for a beachside break to the apartment in Bondi that Hillsong had bought and provided as a parsonage residence. Overseas, the church had acquired other upmarket properties, in which the Houstons would stay as the spirit moved them.

Brian and Bobbie dined with celebrities and politicians, both rising and risen. They stayed in five-star hotels and travelled in style. God had indeed blessed them, and they in turn had brought blessings for God.

So why the pills? And why the booze? Brian Houston spoke at length about his need for sedation in a podcast interview with a fellow evangelical Christian, Canadian pastor Carey Nieuwhof, in 2018. Underlying it all, he claimed, was the long, dark shadow from the past—finding out at the age of 45 that his father, the towering Pentecostal leader Frank Houston, had been a serial paedophile, preying on children in their very own bedrooms.

Here's what Houston said:

'It was in 2012. I really wound down to a place that I genuinely didn't think I could get. My father's story is pretty well known. So when I was forty-five, in 1999, I found out my father had been a paedophile. My father was not only my father. He's my hero, my mentor, and I learnt life and ministry from him. So it was a massive blow, for me, and for a lot of other people as well.

'I was overseeing a whole movement of churches in Australia, eleven hundred churches. I sort of dealt with it at a church level and on a father level in terms of my own children, because this is their granddad. And I dealt with it in all the various levels. But I've probably never, ever really looked after myself, and the grieving and the impact on myself. So from that point—over the next, maybe, ten to twelve years—I think, slowly, I was winding down emotionally.

'And so there was maybe one or two other stressors at the same time. There was a pretty relentless attack for quite a long time, towards me and towards Hillsong Church. And so all of these things, they all worked together to just wind me down on the inside.

'There was another issue that came up at the time, that was personal, close to me, involving someone who I love. And that kind of took me over the top. And so it was—it's the most horrible place to be.'

Houston cited other factors as well. He was travelling inter-nationally and taking sleeping tablets regularly, to the point where he was 'pretty well just totally dependent' on them. He was having panic attacks. One hit him on the night of an appearance he was making at a church on Queensland's Sunshine Coast. He felt that he was unable to breathe. He was convinced his own time was up.

'There were only a few people who really knew the degree of the burnout that I was in. But those people were godsends, the way they supported and stepped into the gap and helped. And obviously, Bobbie, my wife, is a gem. She is just so strong in moments like that. She rises up. And so she was incredible.'

Houston saw a psychologist and a psychiatrist. He was diagnosed with PTSD, relating to the revelations of his father's secret life.

'I think the grace of God . . . that God brought me through and, you know, remarkably quickly. From the position where I was at, where I was a mess, to feeling my old self—it was not a long period of time. Spiralling downwards into it took a long time; I think that period was over twelve years. And then I seemed to bounce out of it. And I don't really even have an explanation for that.

'I honestly think there was a touch of the miraculous about it. Because I was having doctors telling me I'm gonna have to take twelve months off and all the things that normally people would say: that these are panic attacks, that they will become recurring and you'll probably have them for the rest of your life.'

This was typical of Houston's dual messaging. He couldn't have recovered without expert medical help, but really his recovery was another example of God's intervention in his life.

Another constant in the Houston narrative is that Australia was hostile to Hillsong and his work—which contrasted to other parts of the world, including the United States, where 'we get such fair and generally very good media'. He explained it this way in 2015, a year or two before Hillsong reorganised its corporate setup and made for America:

'Australia, for whatever reason . . . I don't know whether it's the tall poppy syndrome, or whether they just don't understand how a church in 2015 could be young and relevant and packed and growing, when all of the statistics would say the church is supposed to be going backwards.

'I find it always disappointing that the Australian media take the stance they take.'

People in the United States might have been more comfortable with the Hillsong style of religious positivity which veered increasingly into the genre of self-improvement. Nevertheless, the shadow of Frank Houston continued to follow his son.

The question of what Brian Houston did with the knowledge he gained in 1999 about his father sat like unexploded ordnance in his life for decades. It emerged dramatically during the hearings of the Royal Commission into Institutional Responses to Child Sexual Abuse, when he was forced to appear as a witness.

The McClellan Inquiry had found that Brian Houston and the National Executive of the Assemblies of God in Australia had not referred allegations of child sexual abuse against Frank Houston to the police. It also found that Brian Houston had a conflict of interest in assuming responsibility for dealing with the allegations of sexual abuse because he was both the national president of the Assemblies of God in Australia and the son of the perpetrator. The inquiry subsequently referred the material to New South Wales authorities.

The matter faded from public view for several years, but roared back in 2021, when Houston was charged by New South Wales police with concealing the crimes of his father.

Behind the shiny façade though there were other dark secrets. Some were financial. Some involved allegations of sexual impropriety by other Hillsong figures.

Most critically, forces were building via a movement of young female Hillsong followers who'd had enough with the old guard of the church who had protected Brian Houston and his inner circle.

In short, Hillsong was to get its own #MeToo movement, leaving Brian Houston exposed as out of touch—and out of time.

Grappling with Hillsong Royalty

Anna Crenshaw might just be the last person you would expect to take a public stand against the Hillsong machine. Her father, Ed Crenshaw, is a respected senior pastor with an evangelical church in Philadelphia. Raised in a Christian home, Anna was lured from the United States to attend Hillsong College at the church's Sydney headquarters. She was following in the footsteps of hundreds of other young Christians from America and around the world, who saw the chance for an adventure in a safe foreign land with sun, surf and the wholesome Hillsong brand.

Anna was only eighteen years old when she arrived in 2016. It wasn't long before she was asked along to a gathering of

Hillsong kids at a house near to Hillsong's headquarters. As the evening wore on, she found herself seated next to a young man who, she recalls, was by now very drunk. He placed his hand on Crenshaw's upper thigh and left it there. She says she just 'froze'.

Meanwhile, another young man at the gathering realised what was happening and offered to take her and other students home. Anna Crenshaw got up to leave. The young man wouldn't let her go.

In a statement she later made to Hillsong, she wrote: 'He grabbed me, putting his hand between my legs and his head on my stomach and began kissing my stomach. I felt his arms and hands wrapped around my legs making contact with my inner thigh, butt and crotch.'

Anna Crenshaw didn't know it at the time, but the young man who had assaulted her was the son of Hillsong royalty. Jason Mays' father, John Mays, was one of the Hillsong originals along with Brian Houston. He had also spent decades as a senior HR employee at Hillsong. Compounding the sin, Jason was married.

Anna Crenshaw was left shaken by Mays' drunken and highly sexual lunge. A counsellor she saw outside the church suggested she could report the perpetrator. It took two and a half years, but eventually, in 2018, she did just that. This was a step which she, as a young foreign student, found 'scary' and 'intimidating'.

In so doing, though, Crenshaw ran into a thicket of old friendships that existed at the very top of the Hillsong hierarchy.

When Crenshaw summoned up the courage to inform Hillsong, she was directed to the church's head of pastoral care oversight, Margaret Aghajanian. Aghajanian is married to George Aghajanian, Hillsong's long-serving general manager, a man who has long been a driving force of Hillsong's success.

According to Anna Crenshaw, when she took her complaint to the church, it took three months to notify Jason Mays of her claim, and then it took no further action for another two months. She says Hillsong only took her complaint seriously and notified the police after her father became involved and pushed the church leaders to act.

Hillsong contests this version of events. It asserts that it only understood how serious the incident was after Crenshaw made 'a formal complaint', four months after she had first provided information about it. Hillsong says it then 'immediately' consulted outside legal counsel.

Anna Crenshaw's concerns, which became a complaint, might not have gone anywhere at all if it not for her own influential family network. Unlike most, Anna Crenshaw had the necessary backing to take on the Houston empire.

Her father, Pastor Ed Crenshaw, called in the support of American evangelical royalty—attorney Boz Tchividjian, who is the grandson of legendary preacher Billy Graham.

In the end, Anna Crenshaw decided to go to the media. She spoke to America's *Vanity Fair* magazine, and its interview with her was published in 2021. Boz Tchividjian—the founder of GRACE (Godly Response to Abuse in the Christian Environment), an organisation dedicated to ending abusive practices in the church—threw his weight behind Anna's decision to speak out against Hillsong; it was, he said, 'a bold step forward in bringing darkness to light' inside the Houstons' church.

Jason Mays was ultimately found guilty of indecent assault at a magistrate's court hearing and was given a two-year good-behaviour bond. No conviction was recorded.

The ordeal scarred Anna Crenshaw, who for years had been a huge fan of Hillsong.

'There's a lot of talk about empowering women, through the work of Bobbie Houston,' she says. 'Yet that wasn't the case when I reported. They spent more time making excuses for the perpetrator.'

Pastor Ed Crenshaw says Hillsong has developed 'a habit of self-protection', citing how the church had treated the victims of Frank Houston.

Anna Crenshaw decided not to let the matter rest with the court finding against Mays. She sued Hillsong for the hurt and pain from the ordeal.

'I feel like they never took any accountability for what happened,' she says. 'And anytime they did talk about what happened, they did so in a way that further hurt me. When I reported, I felt like I was doing the right thing. And I thought, "Okay, now I can move on with my life." I didn't expect it to be years more of them treating me horribly.

'I later learnt there is a phenomenon called betrayal trauma. When you go to your leaders, or the people who are meant to protect you, and they turn a blind eye or don't take it seriously, they make the trauma worse. And I feel like they did that, multiplied by a hundred. And so it really kind of destroyed the life that I had built in Australia.

'But at Hillsong, it was such a hierarchy. And, you know, the people who were in the in-crowd got there by marrying someone who was already in the in-crowd. And it was a lot about power and position. And it was very obvious, as students, that we were not a part of that. And so, for me, that made it a lot harder to report anything.'

Within the tight-knit student community, Anna Crenshaw's case became a symbol of an entrenched culture of insiders and outsiders. It was a potent rallying point for young Christians who had come from other countries and who didn't have local connections. In 2021, the student body put together a lengthy list of grievances that pointed to a culture in which the family and friends of long-term Hillsong figures were given favoured treatment.

Hillsong responded by drawing on the playbook of any corporation facing a reputational crisis: it brought in a high-powered firm of corporate lawyers specialising in crisis management. It was a way of taking action but at the same time keeping damaging information under wraps, under the legal rule of client confidentiality.

Anna Crenshaw would only learn much later that Hillsong had been keeping Brian Houston's own transgressions with two women a secret at the very time when the church was dealing— or failing to deal—with her allegations.

There was evidence, too, of the high-wire act that Brian Houston's life had become. With the moral authority that came with his role as global senior pastor, Houston read out a church statement, in which he publicly chastised Jason Mays for being drunk when he lunged at Anna Crenshaw. '[He] should not have been so drunk that he doesn't even remember the turn of events and it is no excuse for his actions,' was Houston's verdict.

Yet the great moral guardian had himself been forced to admit, in secret, to being so out of it on medications and alcohol that he couldn't remember what had happened when he had spent those 40 minutes in a woman's room at Hillsong's 2019 annual conference.

In the aftermath of Anna Crenshaw's legal action, Boz Tchividjian reflected on what her courageous step showed about Hillsong and other megachurches like it.

'They handled it in a despicable way that seemingly puts the protection of the institution clearly as a priority over the protection and care of the victim, which is, in my opinion, the antithesis of the very gospel they preach,' he says. 'So it was all about institutional self-protection even if that requires the sacrifice of a vulnerable and abused young woman.'

As a former prosecutor, Tchividjian had seen a pattern emerging in cases of sexual abuse.

'I observed something that really troubled me. And that was how many of these cases involve some type of faith community in some fashion,' he said.

The attorney had noted that Hillsong and others in faith communities had what he considered a dualistic world view, which explained why the church tried so hard to keep questions of abuse in-house and away from the authorities.

'The dualistic worldview is us versus them. And "them" is anybody who's not us. And the government is certainly "them". And so why would we go to the government, who is not us? It's them and as the enemy "them" wants to see us destroyed. We're being persecuted by that. So why would we move towards the "them" to report something that occurred within our church family?

'It's really a way to control the narrative. And it's a way to control the situation because so much of these cultures is about control.

'It's not just being abused, but being a victim of a crime. And so one of the very basic things you do—and you could argue this in scriptures, in Romans—is that you report crimes to the governing authorities. But they don't do that because the governing authorities want—in their distorted view, in my opinion—to see their destruction and demise because they're anti-Christian, and they want to persecute the church.'

More Misbehaving Princelings

As Anna Crenshaw's case was playing out in Australia, another scandal was coming to the surface in the United States, also involving the Hillsong old mates' network. By late 2020, Hillsong's New York church was spinning out of control.

That branch's senior pastor, Carl Lentz, had achieved celebrity status and turned the New York version of Hillsong into a holy Hollywood.

'People say we cater to celebrities, and I say, yes, we do,' Lentz said in an interview with GQ. 'Celebrities deserve a relationship with God. Celebrities deserve a place to pray.'

At the top of his pop celebrity list was superstar Justin Bieber, who claimed the church had saved him from his 'dark' days of mental health struggles and drug addiction. It also included Bieber's wife, Hailey Bieber, a model, 'media personality' and socialite, as well as singer and actress Selena Gomez. Lentz had become the personification of Hillsong cool. His schtick was ripped-at-the-knee jeans and torso-hugging T-shirts, teamed with Saint Laurent designer boots at US$1500 a pair.

Lentz was what Hillsong success should look like in the Big Apple. But it also made him a target of PreachersNSneakers, a social media account that lampooned the US prosperity gospel preachers by putting price tags on the exclusive items of clothing they wore on stage. President Donald Trump's trusted pastoral adviser, Paula White, wore US$785 Stella McCartney sneakers; PreachersNSneakers said she was their inspiration and a 'content goldmine'.

It helped the Lentz image that he could cry on stage during a sermon, seemingly at the drop of a hat—and the next day be photographed at the beach with his buff body and perfect wife and kids.

After several years of flying high, Lentz veered too close to the sun. By the end of 2020, he was forced to leave the church after it was revealed, in spectacular tabloid detail, that he was having an extramarital affair. The revelations exploded Lentz's carefully cultivated image as the good Christian family man. With it went the moral authority of Hillsong's main drawcard in the shiny New York market.

His departure ruptured longstanding family ties with the Houstons. As well as partnering with Joel Houston to set up the New York church, Lentz had married Australian woman Laura Brett, the daughter of pastor Kevin Brett, a close friend of the Houstons. Lentz's father, Stephen, had also set up Hillsong's US entities. It was the familiar circle of mates.

Carl Lentz's spectacular fall from grace was a bonfire of wealth, celebrity and excess, brought about by the 'moral failure' of an affair. It also happened to remove the one star in the Hillsong galaxy who burned more brightly than the global senior pastor himself—which perhaps was an even deadlier sin than infidelity in one's marriage.

———

Behind the scenes, another serious scandal was brewing. Allegations of sexual assault had emerged involving another New York pastor.

A junior female staff member of Hillsong New York made an allegation in 2020 that Pastor Reed Bogard had raped her. The alleged rape had occurred in the early days of Hillsong in New York, when Bogard was a founding pastor there, alongside Carl Lentz and Joel Houston.

In the intervening years, Bogard had been assigned away from New York to Hillsong Los Angeles, and had then been promoted to the role of senior pastor of a new Hillsong Church in Dallas, Texas. Bogard was, in other words, part of the elite Hillsong grouping in the United States.

Hillsong commissioned a US law firm, Zukerman Gore Brandeis & Crossman, to investigate the allegations. Its 30-page report was delivered to Hillsong's global board by the beginning of 2021. The findings were damaging for a handful of Hillsong's most senior figures, including Brian Houston, his son Ben Houston, and one of Hillsong's longest-serving and most trusted insiders, Robert Fergusson.

The law firm's report remained secret until it was leaked to me when I was working as investigations editor at the Australian online news site *Crikey* in March 2022. At the time I was receiving more and more leaked information that blew apart Hillsong's highly curated public image.

When the alleged victim complained to Hillsong in 2020, the allegation that she had been raped was new to the church, though the events that had led to it were not.

Hillsong had been told in 2014 that Bogard and the young woman had had an affair. At the time, Hillsong's main concern appeared to be that Bogard was a married man. As far as the church was concerned, this was a moral transgression.

Bogard was taken out of circulation for a number of months. The woman, too, was forced to stand aside from her role. Despite the seriousness (in church terms) of the affair, Bogard was reinstated to duty and then ultimately promoted within the Hillsong USA system.

Senior church members spoke to the woman and to Bogard in 2014, by which time the affair was over. They concluded that it had been consensual at all times. However, in 2020 the young woman revealed something new: that one of the first of their sexual encounters had happened against her will. She alleged that she had twice said 'No' to Bogard before he forced himself on her in the back seat of a car.

It is not known why the young woman made the allegation in 2020. Possibly her decision was influenced by the many revelations of sexual assault and impropriety inspired by the #MeToo movement, and by a heightened awareness of the abuse of power by men in positions of authority.

In its investigation of the rape claim, the law firm judged that the leadership of Hillsong Church Australia, which handled the issue, had failed to conduct 'any meaningful inquiry' back when it became aware of the sexual relationship. It found that the church leadership appeared to 'uniformly assume' that the relationship had been consensual from the outset, even though it involved 'a powerful church leader and a young, low-level staff person'.

The report noted that 'no one at any time ever probed for more information, to try to discern how one of the most powerful men in the New York Church could have found himself in a sexual relationship with a young, vulnerable junior staff member ... And no one appears to have questioned whether meaningful consent was possible, let alone present, given the obvious power dynamic.'

The investigation also pointed to the nature of the sexual activity. It found that the sex that occurred was dictated by the pastor and was marked by a lack of intimacy. It suggested that the acts were 'designed to reinforce the power imbalance between them'. Alarmingly, the investigation also found that Bogard had used his position to force the woman to sign a confidentiality agreement and a non-disparagement clause in her employment contract with the church 'at a time that the affair was in high gear'.

The investigation made observations that cut to the heart of Hillsong's culture of protecting the pastor:

> . . . given the extreme power imbalance between the two, as well as the 'don't say no' culture which permeated the New York Church at that time, there was ample opportunity for Mr. Bogard to take advantage of a systemic inability for [the young woman] to have meaningfully consented at the time in question.
>
> . . . it is likely that a jury, evaluating the interplay, would have found that Mr. Bogard acted without obtaining (or, under the circumstances, having any reasonable expectation of being able to obtain) actual consent. The fact that no Church leader appears to have even considered this issue is a cause for concern.

The investigation was disparaging of the actions of Hillsong elders Robert Fergusson and his wife, Amanda, who conducted the first interview with the woman in 2014. The Fergussons had told the woman she would 'probably lose her job over this'—a statement the law firm found to be 'troublesome', given that there had been no investigation of the circumstances.

The failure to properly investigate the situation tends to call into question the adequacy of any of the limited consequences that resulted from the affair. That leadership would simply take matters as given, without looking into the power dynamics and the specific actions of the participants seems incredible. Certainly such a feeble effort will be unlikely to protect the church from subsequent charges . . .

The investigations delivered a finding that underlined Hillsong's systemic inability to treat women equally: 'More than one witness suggested that it is not uncommon for women to be treated more harshly than men for sexual transgressions.'

This investigation shed light on an entrenched culture of drinking and drug use among the church's leaders in New York. Bogard routinely had seven to eight drinks a night. He claimed to have been drunk at the time of the alleged rape and unable to recall details clearly. He conceded that he had been drunk and was smoking marijuana when he made his first pass at the young woman.

———

Pastor Reed Bogard and his wife, Jess, crashed out of Hillsong in January 2021. They revealed their departure from Hillsong Dallas at the same time as the law firm was sending the report of its investigation to Hillsong.

The Bogards put out a breezy video message, wrapped in familiar Christianese, saying they just needed a change. 'It has been an incredible ride thus far, we've had some crazy days, great days, seeing God do many, many miracles, and we're so grateful for that,' Reed Bogard began. 'With that said, the last ten years of being in church planting mode has really taken a bit of a toll on Jess and I and our family. We just really feel like it's time to transition off of our staff and take some time to remain healthy, get healthy, and really see what this next season holds for us.'

Brian Houston followed up with his own light-on-facts farewell to the couple: 'Reed's announcement to you right now, not sure if that comes as a shock. Reed and Jess have given their heart and soul to the pioneering of Hillsong Dallas. Love the last couple of years, and we're grateful for that, and the great work they've done. Reed and I have been talking now over a period of time and we both agreed it would be a perfect time for them to come to a new season in their life, which means a new season also for Hillsong Dallas.'

Houston made no mention of the legal investigation that had concluded the former staff member's rape claims against Bogard were likely true. Instead, the church allowed an impression to form that the Bogards' removal was all about the misuse of church money, after claims in the US media that the Bogards and other former New York pastors had splurged thousands of dollars on luxury clothes and meals.

In fact, the investigation of Bogard by Zukerman Gore Brandeis & Crossman had come right to the door of Brian Houston himself. It found that the Hillsong founder was involved in the discussions of how to handle the revelations of Bogard's extramarital affair back in 2014. Ben Houston had spoken with

Brian and 'members of the global board' about what the consequences for Bogard should be.

While the investigation provided damaging detail on the culture of Hillsong, it omitted one important fact. Brian Houston and Reed Bogard had a relationship stretching back fifteen years, to the days when Bogard met his future wife, Jess, at Hillsong in Sydney. At that stage, Bogard had been working for Hillsong in a number of different roles. According to information I received, one of those roles brought Bogard into close contact with Brian Houston as Houston's personal driver and an odd-jobs man for the Houston family.

But what no one knew at the time of Bogard's departure in 2021 was that Brian Houston was sitting on his own scandal. Nor was it known that Hillsong was aiding the global senior pastor in keeping it secret.

7
EXODUS

The Music Pastor Pulls the Plug

In 1995 Geoff Bullock's golden association with Hillsong, which had by then lasted twelve years, was drawing to a close. The bitter way it played out became a template for anyone who was seen as a threat to the glory of Hillsong.

Bullock had travelled the world with the Houstons. He knew the character of its global senior pastor inside out. His observation was that Brian Houston had a certain charisma, that people 'wanted to be part of him, to support him', and that they looked to be 'affirmed' by him.

Geoff Bullock was around long enough to see the metamorphosis of Brian Houston from the awkward, somewhat shy and slightly insecure son of Frank to another character altogether. It came about, Bullock says, when Brian travelled to the United States and was in close contact with evangelical preachers who had been moulded by a different culture from Australia's.

As Geoff Bullock saw it, Brian's change in style after his contact with the American megachurch phenomenon was total. Bullock eventually decided to pull the plug on his involvement at Hillsong after realising he no longer shared the church's vision.

He'd already seen firsthand what happened to people with dissenting views. They would get pulled into the office and disciplined. Hillsong didn't tolerate different opinions. They called it 'church discipline', and if you persisted, Bullock recalls, you suddenly weren't on a roster anymore and you had lost your place in the pecking order.

The hardworking music pastor had been staging major live events, week in and week out, across separate locations. The Hillsong crew would perform at a youth meeting on a Saturday night and then pack up their gear. By 5.30 the next morning a truck would arrive to ferry the gear over to Hillsong's main centre, where it would be set up again for the Sunday-morning service.

Bullock was concerned about the toll this was taking on those involved, and especially on the sound crew, who were lugging around huge amounts of gear under constant time pressure. Neither they nor the artists were being paid.

He raised his concerns at a senior pastors' annual retreat with Brian Houston, held at the five-star Ritz-Carlton hotel in Sydney's Double Bay in 1995.

'I was with this group of people that I felt loved by and I loved them deeply,' he says. 'And we were really committed—overcommitted—to supporting Brian's vision and to put up with the hardship of it. And I just said, "Listen, if we keep going this hard, it's gonna break." We were asking these people to contribute. This was a spiritual home for them and they were just working like dogs.'

Houston's reaction, according to Bullock, was sharp.

'He said, "Listen, you're not a union rep, bringing up the whinges and the rights of the workers. Now you're part of management. And you've just got to tell the workers that this is one of the things they've got to do. And if they don't like it, that's fine. Go to another church."'

Houston's take on volunteer labour might have made sense in a smaller, struggling church. But already by 1995 Hillsong's music had taken off worldwide and was set to become the river of gold that would fund the church's expansion.

When Bullock announced in October that he was leaving, he became, instantly, a non-person. His role in Hillsong's rise was so thoroughly erased it was as though he had never been there.

Bullock had just recorded a new album, called *The Other Side*. When he left, he says, the church threw all 5000 CDs into the local tip. 'I went from being the golden boy, so to speak, to being somebody who had been excommunicated. They started to get staff to sign non-disclosure agreements. And I was told that, if I got in touch with anybody, then they had to report to Brian what I'd said. I lost all my friends, I lost all my contacts, and I had to start again. They declared war on me.'

Bullock was persona non grata for years. What happened to him has been repeated again and again in Hillsong. The golden rule is do not rock the boat. Do not make trouble—and that

means not reporting possible criminal behaviour to the authorities. Because nothing can get in the way of spreading the word
of Jesus.

The Start of a Perilous Descent

Hillsong's treatment of college student Anna Crenshaw crystal-
lised a fundamental truth about its project: there is a special
clique of people at the top who play by different rules from the
rest. A select group of Houston family and friends could seemingly do as they pleased, with the protection of an old boys'
network at the top.

For some, this was the very antithesis of the Christian
message. Perhaps it is the logical end point when a religious
movement is hijacked by a greed-is-good ethos.

Thirty years or so after it started in the Hills District of
Sydney, Hillsong was beginning its terminal descent.

You could always buy your way into the top tier at Hillsong.
Apart from the Kingdom Builders donation scheme, which gave
donors access, there was also a special networking group called
Business Connect, which encouraged 'managers' and 'executives' to sit around a boardroom table together at the offices of
one of Hillsong's board members who happens to be a chartered
accountant.

And with enough money, you could rub shoulders with God's
anointed one, Global Senior Pastor Brian Houston.

There was even a VIP section at Sunday church gatherings. Who ever heard of such a thing? But in the money- and
prestige-soaked culture of Hillsong, it was unremarkable.

With the passing of the years, a new generation was rising to take over the empire. But there was nothing new about this group. They were the so-called legacy kids: the privileged sons and daughters of the church founders. They were the new ruling elite, the inheritors of Hillsong's wealth and power.

But they were to meet their match in a small group of Christian women who were disgusted by what they saw and cared enough about their faith to do something about it.

Fiona Jones is one of these women, and she remembers very clearly the night her illusions about Hillsong were shattered. It was the moment she describes as 'the beginning of the end'.

'I had been invited to a New Year's Eve party at Joel Houston's old house in Bondi,' she recalls. 'I wasn't long out of high school. The Bible college had a very strict policy for youth leaders with alcohol, with sex. You know, it was very highly conservative.

'I walked in and the room was filled with the Hillsong "who's who": the young people who appeared on albums and, you know, some of them even preached on weekends. They were all legacy kids, so their parents were prominent figures of Hillsong.

'Everyone there was absolutely sloshed. And it was at this moment that I was really confused because I was, like, "What? What is happening here?"

'I saw a staff member who was married and her clothes were sort of falling off. She was dancing with someone who wasn't her husband. And I remember going to the bathroom and there were loads of people in there. Obviously there were weird things happening. I saw drugs.

'And I felt so uncomfortable I just left the party. I hopped on the bus, and never told anyone, but just came home.'

The behaviour which Fiona Jones witnessed was the very opposite of the purity doctrine which was enforced upon the young people who were attracted to Hillsong.

'The emphasis of youth camps and youth events and Friday-night youth group was that your devotion to God is shown in how you abstain from substances and abstain from sex,' she explains. 'But here they were doing the opposite.

'It was clear that this particular group of people didn't have integrity. And that was the beginning of [my] seeing that there were rules for some that didn't apply to everyone. And it was just like a moment of my innocence going. I think I was shattered because these were the people I watched on Hillsong DVDs, talking about wanting to make a difference and about having a devout faith.'

While there was favoured treatment for an inner circle of Hillsong, the women discovered there was a well-developed system for silencing dissent. Another young woman, Helen Smith, saw direct lessons from the treatment of Anna Crenshaw.

'For a lot of us, when you have this #MeToo movement happening, when you have the broader evangelical church being okay with Donald Trump and his behaviour, you see more and more how your voice never did matter within Pentecostal churches,' Helen says. 'And then you see the Anna Crenshaw thing, when you see that Brian seems to have not wanted to acknowledge what his behaviour represents in how he treated women.

'I said to my husband at one point—particularly when the Jason Mays and Anna Crenshaw thing blew up—that I wasn't sure that I was okay with taking my kids to church, which is what I grew up expecting I would do. I didn't see it as a safe place anymore for me or my children. The way they handle serious allegations, they think that they're above the law.'

Fiona Jones saw the silencing of dissent on several levels.

'I think the thing that shocked me was just being told explicitly by another woman that, if I wanted to get anywhere, then there were rules I had to follow. You can't complain about the sexual abuse, you can't complain about the racism, you can't complain about the free labour you give through volunteering. They looked at it as though they gave you the opportunity, so you owe them everything. And how dare you speak out against God's anointed?'

Anita Clarke survived a similar experience to Anna Crenshaw. She, too, took her complaint to the top of Hillsong but ran into a dead end.

'My complaint was about a pastor,' Anita explains. 'I was told that I'm an adult and that I'm responsible for my own heart to goodness. I was told I can't make Hillsong pastors look bad, because that makes the church look bad. And the church is Jesus. It's all about Jesus. So you're attacking God.

'I mean, Brian, used the term "God haters", about people speaking out about the church, in a tweet. He tweeted about the gossips and the God haters.'

It was becoming apparent that a two-tiered system operated

at Hillsong. There were insiders and outsiders. Different rules applied depending on who you knew.

The discrimination built into the system was repellent for those who took their religious beliefs seriously. It was younger women in particular who could no longer abide the hypocrisy of the church leadership.

Quietly a small group was forming fired by the desire to bring change to Hillsong, starting at the top.

Hillsong Versus the 21st Century

The world had changed a great deal in the four decades since Hillsong set up shop in the aspirational, white, middle-class suburbs of the Hills District. Hillsong itself, though, had not. Nor had the broader Pentecostal movement.

In Ipswich, near Brisbane, Trudy Rogers encountered a solid block of paternalism at her Pentecostal church.

'When I was one of the women's leaders and led a fair number of ladies' groups, the church board was comprised of twelve men,' she notes. 'It sort of struck me that this didn't seem very balanced. You know, why is there not even a single woman on the board?

'I didn't know if it was church policy or whether it just happened that way. So I approached the senior pastor one day and sort of tackled him about it. And I couldn't believe his reply, because he just said, "Well, Trudy, I don't know any women who are innovative enough thinkers to put on the board."

'And while I'm sort of doing a bit of a double-take, he added, as a sort of consolation, that while he felt that I was an innovative thinker, he didn't think I would be interested in being on the board.'

The men-only Pentecostal club that Trudy Rogers encountered confirmed both the spirit and the letter of the governance model that had operated at Frank Houston's original Sydney megachurch, where good men were defined by the Bible in the verses of Timothy and Titus. Qualifications for a Houston board member included that 'He is to be blameless or above reproach', he is to be 'the husband of one wife' and he is to 'rule his house well'.

Trudy Rogers was then in her late forties. She recalled that all the senior pastors were male. She describes a setup which sounds like it was in 1950, but was in fact in the year 2000. It has changed little since. 'Submission to leadership was very much emphasised,' she says. 'And the way they managed to get the household or authority structure in place was that they used the scripture, where it says "wives submit to your husbands and husbands love your wives".'

At Hillsong, two decades on, Fiona Jones confronted the same disjunction between the outside world and the world of the evangelical bubble. 'I just was absolutely shocked at how many white men were in charge,' she says. 'There was just a massive lack of diversity, both with people of colour and women.'

So what is a woman meant to do at Hillsong, where nearly every board member and every senior manager for the last 30 years has been male and an old friend of the Houstons?

The answer is: be like Bobbie.

Bobbie Houston—or Mumma Dove, as she came to be affectionately known—built a whole new branch of Hillsong called the Colour Sisterhood, representing what Hillsong women should be. She was the yin to Brian's yang.

For four decades, Brian and Bobbie Houston were the royalty at the top of Hillsong, the happily married husband-and-wife team. They radiated contentment with their prosperous lives and their solid family values. They were also a living example of the complementarianism that is at the heart of successful male–female coupling at Hillsong, modelling for the congregation how couples should be and how mums and dads should raise their kids.

Many of those who lost their faith in Hillsong, however, came to see the perfect husband-and-wife team as a perfect deception.

Says Helen Smith: 'I realised that I probably saw what I wanted to see while I was in [Hillsong]. Now, looking at it, you realise that the wife and woman role is so tokenistic. Like, you know, there'll be the youth pastors and the wife is named, even though she's got really no authority.'

Fiona Jones saw the picture-perfect husband-and-wife pastor team as a giant fig leaf, hiding an entrenched system of gender roles and discrimination. 'So they are fine to parade women out and say, "Look we have a women's conference. Look we have women preaching,"' she notes. 'But you need to present yourself in a certain way. And you don't have agency [over] what kind of woman you can be in Hillsong.

'There are jokes about how every woman in Hillsong dresses the same, especially the women on staff. They all wear these long kimonos. They have Tiffany bracelets. They have the big white watch that Bobbie Houston wears. They all straighten their hair, even if they've got curly hair. They all wear leather boots that are high-heeled. It's a very strong archetype.

'And you have to be funny and sexy. And all of these things at once. You know, if you want to be overweight, if you want to be a girl who doesn't wear make-up, or doesn't straighten her hair, you're not gonna get ahead and become, you know, the pastor's wife.

'These women had a Thursday-morning meeting where you sit down and Bobbie tells you how to be the perfect woman. And you're literally there writing down, you know, all of these tips and tricks Bobbie's telling you. Like how to age gracefully and embrace your wrinkles and your greys. Bobbie has [had] all this work done on her face, and she's sitting there talking to suburban women who don't make a six-figure salary or whatever. They try to impress upon you that, if you just walk with God, He renews your youth. When I see Bobbie's face, I'm thinking, "That is not God's work."

'Inclusion is not equality. Inclusion is token and it reflects well on them. But the question is: what kind of woman gets ahead at Hillsong? And how far can she even go anyway? It's the campus pastor model. Hillsong usually pays the man and expects the woman to be a full-time volunteer. So even the pay and labour gap is huge.'

Fiona came to see the Bobbie Houston–inspired role that was assigned to women in the church as being that of an enabler: 'So you've got this version of a caste system. There are rewards. It's like the days of the plantation, where you had the house slave who was given rewards, you know, like sleeping in the house, being able to do domestic tasks. His role was to control the field slaves, to go out and say, "Don't be obstinate, don't rock the boat."

'That's the function of these women in relation to women's progress.'

———

For every young woman who quietly shifted her allegiance away from the Houstons, there was a point of no return.

Helen Smith had been raised in a Christian family but found Hillsong's excesses to be too much. 'For me, as a Christian, I had been attracted to the person of Jesus, who sat with the poor, sat with the people who were socially unacceptable at the time,' she explains. 'He was someone who went into churches and overthrew temples and told religious leaders off. I like the idea of someone who would sit with the woman at the well, even though that was culturally wrong. I read the gospels and I read about a person who didn't go for opulence. Hillsong was actually the antithesis of Jesus and the gospel. So I think it just seemed to be the complete opposite end of the spectrum of what my faith was.'

For Helen, the breaking point was what she calls the 'entitlement' of Brian Houston and his close family. Helen came to know of the personal errands that were being done for the Houston family using staff paid by the church. Helen became aware of Brian Houston's outbursts if he considered his home hadn't been properly cleaned. 'I stopped giving to the church because I didn't think my tithe should be paid for Brian to have a pool cleaner and a gardener,' she says.

Anita Clarke learnt what it was like to suddenly fall out of favour.

'If you're out, you are out,' she says. 'I was floating along in the inner circles for so long I didn't realise what it was like to be in an outer circle. Or that you can go from being inside to out. And it's not about being angry or being bitter about that, because, ultimately, it was a gift to be pushed out. And once I had more insight into those relationships, I realised that it was all built on something false anyway.'

For Fiona Jones, many things converged at once.

'More and more I was surrounded by these people who were haters and racist and misogynistic,' she says. 'And increasingly for me [it] was against what I fundamentally understand to be Christianity. There was favouritism, and then it went beyond favouritism. It's nepotism. It's cronyism. It's covering up of sexual abuse. It's the treatment of women. It's the treatment of people of colour, and it's being upheld by this theology I don't believe in.'

For those who are not of the church, it can be almost impossible to understand the horrific emotional toll it takes on a member to move away from their Christian community. Speaking publicly about it means you will likely be cut off for good. And then there's the guilt and the fear. The Old Testament Book of Deuteronomy holds that those who might cause others to abandon their faith should be punished by death—an unlikely consequence in the 21st century but a pointer to the gravity for some of the act of leaving.

A young Sydney woman named Monique Rafton wrote her master's thesis on what it was like to be an 'exvangelical' after leaving Hillsong and churches like it. Rafton had shifted to Hillsong from an Anglican church because Hillsong allowed women to preach, and, in Pentecostal fashion, because it emphasised the Holy Spirit. 'I was desperate to feel God, to make him tangible rather than an abstract concept,' she explains.

Monique enrolled in a year of full-time Bible study at Hillsong College where, she says, the all-consuming environment perhaps extended her faith by a year or two. But when she left college to travel overseas, she began to perceive the world in a different light.

'I was studying abroad, outside of the bubble that I grew up in, and the toxic debate surrounding the same-sex marriage plebiscite exposed an ugliness within the Australian Christian landscape,' she says. It spurred her academic work, *Losing My Religion*, on the 'rising phenomenon of the "Exvangelical" movement in Australia'.

Her thesis found that the two main reasons former members of evangelical churches gave for leaving were their intellectual doubt over the veracity of Christianity's claims, and their moral criticisms of its teachings and norms, particularly as these related to women, the LGBTIQA+ community, sex and purity culture, sexual abuse and colonialism.

Coming to a new realisation about these matters was one thing. Leaving the church, for Monique and others, was and is something else.

'It took some time to reveal to my Christian family and friends that I no longer believed; by far the hardest part of my deconversion was knowing that they now believed I was destined for hell,' she says.

For years Brian Houston had demonised the secular media, depicting it as damaging the church. Imagine, then, the courage it has taken for women to go outside the sanctioned and sanctified space of Hillsong and to risk the destruction of all they know to speak out about their experiences. And yet they did.

8
THE END TIMES

Brian's Fall

By the beginning of 2022, the dark clouds had well and truly gathered over the Hillsong enterprise. The scandals had banked up. The past was catching up.

In the United States, Brian Houston's New York campus had imploded. His star preacher and family friend Carl Lentz had caused an almighty spectacle with a very public moral implosion. Reed Bogard, another of the founding New York pastors—and a one-time personal staffer to Brian Houston—had been moved on, with allegations of rape against him, which had been kept secret. (Bogard has not been charged with any offenses.)

Separately, the Anna Crenshaw matter, which started in Australia, had seeped over to the United States, where the respectable and reputable end of the American evangelical movement had swung in behind the Crenshaws and against Brian Houston. The reaction was led by lawyer Boz Tchividjian, who—apart from being Billy Graham's third-eldest grandchild and Professor of Law at the evangelical Liberty University—is a former chief prosecutor and the founder and executive director of the church reform organisation GRACE.

In mid-2021 in Australia, New South Wales police charged Brian Houston with the crime of concealing information on sexual abuse committed by his father, Frank Houston. The ghost of more than twenty years past had finally returned; Houston had learnt of his father's crimes back in 1999. As a result of the police charge, Houston temporarily stood aside from Hillsong business.

Behind the scenes, the rumbling thunder was coming closer to home. By early 2022, unknown to the wider church community, some Hillsong elders had become uneasy about new information that had surfaced about Brian Houston's past. With Houston having stepped aside, the veil was lifted on some closely held secrets.

Hillsong's elders are the church's most illustrious figures; some date their association with the church back to its earliest days. They are meant to act as spiritual counsellors and to provide wise advice to the church. But they were now hearing disturbing details about Brian Houston's behaviour for the first time.

Brian Houston had been hitting the bottle—again. Word was starting to leak out that he had a drinking problem. He had been seen out and about drunk in his old haunt of Bondi. What seemed impossible was shaping as a reality: the bad old days of pills and booze were back, and the indomitable Brian Houston was teetering on the edge.

The church leadership proposed to put out a statement that was light on detail about Brian Houston's past sins and his substance-abuse problems. It would focus on the need for him to take time out and look after his health. But there came a point where some church elders were no longer happy with what amounted to a cover-up of Houston's activities.

By early 2022, the dissent had grown louder within the church. That's when an anonymous email regarding behind-the-scenes ructions at Hillsong arrived in my inbox one Monday night in the middle of March. By the end of the week, this email had proven to be remarkably well informed. The truth—or something resembling it—would be flushed out, and Hillsong's attempted cover-up blown away.

Hillsong refused to be drawn on the gathering crisis. It never engages, which can make observing Hillsong a little like watching the Kremlin or the Vatican. Sometimes you only discover that a major ruction is occurring because of a whisper here or there. The organisation rarely, if ever, comes clean with full and frank answers. It manages information as if it is a large corporation— which of course it is. Hillsong is very good at controlling the narrative and minimising the damage to its brand.

Official silence might be the church's tactic of choice, but elsewhere in Hillsong Land the whispers built to a roar with the unexplained disappearance from the church's website of the entire list of elders. Rumour had it that one or more of those elders now held serious moral concerns about Brian Houston's behaviour. I sought to confirm these rumours with church elders.

One was Dr Gordon Lee, a general practitioner from Sydney. Dr Lee had been a church loyalist for decades and had always been there for the church's big moments, such as when Hillsong elders met in 2000 to consider how to handle the information they had received about Frank Houston's sexual abuse of boys.

The doctor promotes the Christian values of his medical practice via his online profile:

To glorify God by building medical practices that deliver
high quality holistic care. Values:
1. *A love for God*
2. *A love for His Church*
3. *A love for People.*

So it was no surprise, when I contacted him, that the Hillsong elder was reluctant to confirm that he held moral concerns about his church's leadership. According to the doctor's receptionist, he 'does not want to discuss it because Dr Lee says the church is his family'.

When I contacted Hillsong, they refused to be drawn on the gathering crisis. However, the church now knew that the story of Brian Houston's drinking and alleged moral transgression involving a female Hillsong supporter was about to come out in the media. Rather than confirm or deny the information, Hillsong took the pre-emptive step of calling an all-staff meeting.

For those who know Hillsong, this was a familiar strategy. Say nothing, act in secret and then put out your own version of events as a public comment on the Hillsong website. But this time there were several close observers who were determined that the church would not control the public narrative. And the best way to do that, they judged, was to record the staff meeting and immediately send the recording to an interested journalist.

———

On Friday, 18 March 2022 at 9.30 am, a Zoom meeting began, the purpose being to inform staff of news on Brian Houston. Thirty minutes later, a recording of the proceedings reached me via a secure email.

The recording captures the biggest moment in the church's 40-year history: the moment when Hillsong announced it was the end of the line for the church's charismatic founder and leader, Pastor Brian Houston.

The video also stands as an extraordinary example of how the church justifies covering up for the most powerful in its ranks—a perverse exercise in religion-informed logic, which finds justification for protecting the perpetrator and punishing those who speak up.

Thrust forward for this moment was Senior Pastor Phil Dooley, by now in his early fifties. On the tape, he is a paragon of Hillsong chic, with golden locks tumbling to his shoulders and the obligatory baseball cap giving him the look of a man half his age.

Among the faces along the top of the Zoom screen was one very special onlooker, Bobbie Houston. Wearing her own distinctive blue cap bearing the number '7', she kept her head down as she listened closely to Pastor Phil's address and took notes on behalf of her absent husband.

Completing the picture was Hillsong's general manager, George Aghajanian, the American-accented executive who had been spearheading the Hillsong project for decades as the organisational right-hand man to Brian Houston. Aghajanian, it appears from the recording, has little time for fashion. He is there to protect the business.

Pastor Phil Dooley was born and raised in the dead-ordinary environs of the Hills District, and educated at the local state high school. The day he walked into Hillsong changed his life and set him on a path to success, and not a small degree of wealth, as a pastor with experiences which took him and Lucinda, his wife and co-pastor, around the world. Their last stop had been South Africa, where the Dooleys had pastored to an outpost of the empire.

Now he had the task of taking down a legend.

Pandora's Box

Unsurprisingly, the meeting began with tears.

'We have such an incredible church of amazing faithful people,' Pastor Phil began with wavering voice, before checking himself briefly. 'At the start of this year, there was an announcement made by Pastor Brian that he would be stepping aside for twelve months, for the reason of his own personal health and emotional wellbeing and because of the court case that he is going to be dealing with at the end of the year. And Lucinda and I were asked to step into this interim role.

'And the reason why he took that step is absolutely the truth,' he added.

The interim senior pastor was about to reveal long-held secrets on the behaviour of Brian Houston. Call it a controlled explosion.

The first incident had taken place some ten years before, around 2013. This involved Brian Houston text messaging with a female member of staff. '[It] ended in an inappropriate text message along the line of, "If I was with you, I'd like to give you a kiss and a cuddle, or a hug," words of that nature,' Phil Dooley said. 'That particular staff member was obviously upset by that and felt awkward, and I think responded to that, went to George Aghajanian and decided that she would like to leave staff because of that. And so she did.'

The second incident, he said, had taken place in 2019, during Hillsong's annual conference, the church's big set-piece event featuring celebrity pastors from Australia and the United States, and which attracts tens of thousands to Sydney's Olympic Park stadium.

Here, after a long day, Brian Houston had been drinking at the bar of the Pullman Hotel with a group of Hillsong people, with drinks finishing late at night. The group included a woman who was a major donor to Hillsong via the Kingdom Builders scheme. She had paid her fee to attend the conference.

'Later that evening,' Dooley began—and then interrupted himself to note that 'Brian had also been taking anxiety tablets'. Dooley resumed: 'And later that evening, he [Pastor Brian] went to attempt to go to his room. Didn't have his room key, and ended up knocking on the door of this woman's room. And she opened the door, and he went into her room.

'The truth is, we don't know exactly what happened next. This woman has not said that there was any sexual activity. Brian has said there was no sexual activity. But he was in the room for forty minutes. He doesn't have much of a recollection because of, he says, the mixture of the anxiety tablets and the alcohol.

'This woman had also been drinking. And so her recollection is not completely coherent. So, based on that, that happened. This particular woman then felt, obviously, a whole lot of conflicting emotions. She then went and spoke to someone on staff, who then spoke to someone, I think, ultimately went to Brian and Brian referred it to George [Aghajanian].'

The revelation that a drunk Brian Houston had lost his room key and somehow then ended up spending 40 minutes in a woman's hotel room was news that immediately grabbed headlines, in Australia and internationally.

Of itself, the revelation was enough to end Brian Houston's association with the church. It also caused massive ructions among pastors in the United States. Little wonder, then, that the church leadership had kept it secret for three years, and had further tried to keep a lid on it when it became known to the church elders.

———

Phil Dooley's 30-minute announcement contained much else that illuminates how Hillsong operates when confronted with events that might threaten its authority or its reputation. As a full and frank mea culpa, it fell well short. Indeed, it raised more questions than it answered.

First and foremost was the central role of the Hillsong leadership group in taking no action over Houston's errant behaviour. In both the 2013 and 2019 incidents, it emerged, they had known of Houston's actions and had been party to keeping them secret.

In both cases, complaints made by the women were dealt with solely by the men dispatched by the church. In 2019 Hillsong carried out an 'investigation', which the church claimed was independent but which was in fact carried out by a group of men, all of whom had longstanding close ties to Brian Houston.

In addition to the investigative team from the church's so-called 'integrity unit', there were two 'outsiders', associates of Brian Houston.

One member of the leadership group had been particularly keen to point out during the church's disclosure session that Brian Houston had on both occasions been affected by sleeping tablets or anti-anxiety medication, and also mounted a strong attack on Hillsong's elders, some of whom he accused of spreading gossip, though in fact they had simply raised questions about the church's response.

'The global board is tasked with the responsibility of overseeing all of our pastors—the credentialling, the disciplining, the restoration process,' he said. 'Not the elders. The elders' role is to basically pray for people, and to care for people spiritually. But beyond that, they have no governance authority in our church.

'And yet a very few of them are speaking as if they have a lot of authority. And the reality is that it's the global board's responsibility to make sure that, when situations arise—whether it's with any of our pastors, or Pastor Brian—we abide by our code of conduct and our disciplinary restoration process.

'As a church right now, or as a staff right now, we have to pull together in unity and allow the global board to work through these situations. And having voices from all around contributing into this equation is unhelpful, and is going to hurt our church significantly. And it's going to hurt Brian, Bobbie and the family.'

It emerged that the church's leadership had debated 'back and forth' about how to deal with the news of the 2019 scandal, as well as with Houston's recent drunkenness. It had been initially decided, Dooley said, that a public statement would be put out that 'focused on where he was at with regard to his own health and emotional needs to get better and the court case', and that this would be done 'without mentioning these other issues'. In other words, Hillsong initially proposed to keep Houston's transgressions involving women secret.

Dooley conceded that this could look like a cover-up, but argued that it wasn't: 'In these situations . . . with the evidence that was before the global board, the decision was made to offer, I suppose, what I would call grace, and not to cover up, but to not expose,' he reasoned.

'Grace' was, at this moment, the *mot du jour* for the senior pastor.

'And we, I think, as a church, we have always been a church that sees the grace of God expressed in Jesus,' he continued.

'And ... our desire is not to expose anyone, but to give people room to be restored, and to give people room to repent, and to move forward, and to have the right people know, and the right people offer accountability, and a process to move forward to health and community.'

Dooley was also able to offer as an authority the Biblical figure of Timothy, in Timothy 5:19–20, to support not revealing the truth about Houston's actions.

'If you look at Timothy—when do you publicly expose someone's sin? He talks about that happening when someone's behaviour is such that they're not at a position where they are under any form of accountability, where they are basically working against the church. There's just no space for them to be in any fellowship. And they're working really in opposition to it.'

According to Dooley's formulation of church discipline, Brian Houston, as a perpetrator, deserved to be handled with kid gloves and to have his transgressions kept quiet. Anyone questioning Houston's actions, on the other hand, was a troublemaker—and certainly not part of the 'fellowship'.

As far as the public was concerned, no action was taken by the Hillsong leadership group against Houston.

———

We have never heard from the two women in question about what Brian Houston really did. The only version of events was that which Hillsong decided to make public. The women caught up in Houston's behaviour have been, quite literally, voiceless.

According to the Hillsong version, the recipient of Houston's inappropriate and unwelcome text messaging in 2013 had apparently 'wanted to leave her job' after speaking with George Aghajanian. A short time later she contacted Hillsong to say she was having trouble finding work. She told the church that she felt it was 'unfair' that she had to leave her job the way she did. She asked for some compensation. Hillsong gave her 'a couple of months' salary' to get on with. In the Zoom meeting, Pastor Dooley made a point of saying that Brian Houston said he would pay.

The woman who was caught up in Houston's drunken approach in 2019 had wanted action from the board. She has never said if she was happy with the result, although it is known that she has left the church, having previously been a major donor. At her request, Hillsong repaid her conference fee, as well as her Kingdom Builder donation.

As far as is publicly known, the police have never been involved. Was there any serious independent inquiry into what occurred?

Hillsong's response was consistent with the pattern it had established decades before with its treatment of Brett Sengstock: keep the matter in-house, pay the least you can in compensation, and protect the church at all costs.

Holy Moses

It was unimaginable that Brian Houston, the founder and figure-head of the Hillsong phenomenon, could fall, but fall he did, having been pushed out by the Hillsong board—in the name of creating a 'healthy' church, as it was styled. The removal of the founder and global senior pastor would open the floodgates in a way the church had never experienced before.

The inner workings of the Hillsong money-machine were about to be exposed in a devastating blow that would bring to light financial truths the Houstons' followers had never known.

As young female dissidents who had left Hillsong mobilised quietly behind the scenes, another woman still inside the church, Natalie Moses, was preparing to make a very loud noise indeed. She would become the first-ever insider to blow the whistle on the behaviour of the church's most senior figures. Her revelations came crashing out in the aftermath of Brian and Bobbie Houston's departure, and were driven, in part, by her disgust at how the church had buried the truth on Brian Houston's transgressions involving women.

Natalie Moses and her husband, Glen, had been part of the Hillsong scene in the Hills District for three years or so before Natalie took up a role managing the church's governance—a position that gave her access to information on the money flows into and out of the church.

Natalie and Glen had been drawn into the Hillsong milieu by their teenage daughter. It was a familiar path: the parents joining up with Hillsong because of their kids, who were attracted by the church's music and its vibe. The Moses family had even packed up their home and moved across Sydney to be closer to the Hillsong mothership. Their daughter had decided she wanted to attend Hillsong College rather than go to university. They ended up renting 200 metres from the campus.

Natalie and Glen were committed Christians. The two had met at a Church of Christ gathering and were united in their desire to do good in the world. 'Once you realise that your actions can make such a difference to someone else's life, you never feel the same again,' says Glen. 'For me it was intoxicating.'

They had contemplated a life as Christian missionaries working overseas, but then Natalie fell pregnant. They put their plans to move to Mexico on hold and decided to stay in Sydney and look for work that would allow them to express their religious compassion and be paid. Natalie worked with various religious charities, including Catholic Mission and Samaritan's Purse, an evangelical Christian organisation that provides aid to people in need around the world. Glen, too, worked for Samaritan's Purse and helped out on relief efforts in Puerto Rico after the island was devastated by hurricanes in 2017.

While they had been deeply involved in evangelical Christianity, neither had been part of the Pentecostal church before making the move to Hillsong. They tried to fit in as much as possible, with Glen joining several Hillsong 'connect' groups before finding the right one. He also served as an unpaid helper at church on Sundays.

Natalie Moses was employed at Hillsong from March 2020 as a fundraising and governance coordinator, which involved her in raising donation revenues, increasing 'donor engagement', making grant applications and managing the reporting of church income. This put her at the very heart of the Hillsong enterprise: the getting of money. Critically, she also had access to board papers, minutes of meetings, and resolutions for several Hillsong entities stretching back around ten years.

Natalie brought an outsider's eye—and the experience of years in other charities—to an organisation that had been run by a small clique of Houston family and friends. She discovered a laundry list of financial transactions between Hillsong entities and involving senior Hillsong figures that she considered legally questionable.

In the past, Hillsong staffers might have looked the other way. Over decades, loyal workers had trusted the Hillsong project and accepted the culture of not rocking the boat.

But Natalie Moses was motivated by her strong sense of how a Christian organisation should act—qualities that should worry any church with dirty secrets to keep. She had also been watching on as the scandal around Brian Houston's drunken visit to the woman's hotel room in 2019 unfolded.

Over a period of two years, Natalie Moses became increasingly concerned about the legality of financial transactions she became privy to. Her concerns about money flows within the church escalated around the time news of the scandal broke in March 2022 concerning Brian Houston's behaviour with two women.

Having been stung by revelation after revelation in the media, Hillsong's leadership was on high alert. After the departure of Brian Houston the church set about hunting down the source of leaks to the media—despite publicly declaring it had entered a new phase where there would be no more secrets.

In a subsequent court filing the church disclosed that after an IT investigation its five-man group of senior managers concluded 'it was possible' that Natalie Moses 'could have been providing information to media reporters'. This was based on a finding that Moses had downloaded 'a significant number of documents and files' including documents that contained 'confidential and sensitive information' that 'may not be connected' with her role.

By June 2022 Moses' access to Hillsong's computers and shared files was cut. She was soon suspended, amid threats from Hillsong that it would refer the case to the police.

Moses insisted that she had downloaded work files—alleged by Hillsong to number more than 40,000—to enable her to perform her job. She later started legal action against Hillsong claiming she was victimised and treated unfairly by church management after making her governance concerns known. Her legal team alleged that the church victimised her because it 'believed or suspected' that she 'may have made, proposed to make, or could make a disclosure' that qualified for protection under whistleblower legislation.

The case of Moses versus Hillsong headed to the Federal Court in 2022, just months after Houston's fall. The insider was now claiming whistleblower status.

Hillsong's most sensitive secrets were now in the hands of those it perceived as enemies.

———

So what did Natalie Moses find that was so devastating? According to her Federal Court claim, Moses discovered irregularities in the transfer of funds from Hillsong's Australian entities.

It started with her concern about how $10,000 was to be passed to people seeking to establish a Hillsong Church in Romania. Moses warned her boss that overseas transfers of this type were not permitted under the legislation governing not-for-profit organisations in Australia. The funds were eventually paid via a United States–based Hillsong entity, thereby avoiding the Australian regulations.

From there, Moses, according to her statement of claim, briefed Hillsong's directors on the need for better compliance of the church's eighteen not-for-profit entities in Australia. This included creating agreements for third-party transfers, including to its international operations, and creating a system to manage conflicts of interest in a formal way. This would have meant that transactions between the dozens of Hillsong corporate entities in Australia and America, most of which had common directors, would be transparent.

Moses says she made her concerns known via a presentation to departmental heads at Hillsong HQ. She detailed the changes that she said needed to be made, including meeting the external conduct standards demanded by the regulator on sending money overseas.

Moses' statement of claim also revealed that Australia's charities regulator, the Australian Charities and Not-for-profits Commission (ACNC), had been quietly investigating Hillsong's compliance with the charity laws. Natalie Moses had been assigned by Hillsong to work with the investigation team in early 2022, before she blew the whistle four months later. The regulator was looking into the operations of ten Hillsong charities. Two had the special status of Basic Religious Charities, and therefore had not been required to reveal any information about their finances. (The regulator, incredibly, is prevented by law from stating publicly that it is investigating an organisation.)

Moses' statement of claim goes on to say that, when she revealed her findings to Hillsong's senior ranks, she was told to 'come up with a story' that would be acceptable to investigators from the ACNC.

Collectively, Natalie Moses' disclosures point to small fortunes being paid to a select group of pastors in the Hillsong organisation. There are several eye-catching details in her statement.

Moses alleged that a number of directors of Hillsong Church were classified as pastors and were being paid full-time salaries, as well as receiving large tax-free honorariums for speaking at Hillsong Churches globally. Funds were allegedly being transferred between entities in the Hillsong global group with little to no discussion of what was in the best interests of those entities. Significant gifts were also made to directors of Hillsong companies and their families and friends.

Natalie Moses had suggested that there needed to be a wider internal audit to cover conduct involving senior Hillsong executives, including close friends of the Houstons. She alleged that she had discovered large cash gifts and designer gifts that were provided to Brian Houston and his family, friends, board directors and their family members.

Finally, she alleged that Hillsong's chief financial officer, Peter Ridley, had declared that God would protect Hillsong during the ACNC's investigation, as 'God protects the righteous and Hillsong is the righteous'. (Hillsong specifically denied this allegation, along with several other claims made by Moses.)

Natalie Moses' allegations were an echo of just about every finding from the US Senate inquiry conducted by Senator Chuck Grassley in 2011.

Watching from the United States, Barry Bowen, the religious rorts researcher from the Texas-based Trinity Foundation, was gobsmacked by the similarities to claims made against US televangelists, down to the honorarium system of pastors paying their friends large amounts of tax-free money to speak at their churches.

'There are four stages in the church and ministry money cycle,' he says. 'And a different form of fraud or theft can happen at any stage. The first is when you ask for money. The fraud is when or if you misrepresent where the money will go. Second is the collection stage, and whether or not there is any skimming off the top. Third is the depositing of funds. The fraud is if dedicated funds don't go to the fund which the donor intended. Finally, there is the reporting stage, where Hillsong needs to provide a complete accounting of where the money is going. Natalie Moses' allegations cover all those.'

Moses' disclosures constituted a huge threat to the Hillsong enterprise. They raised serious questions about how the church complied with the charities law in Australia. And if the church failed to comply, then that raised the key question of whether or not Hillsong should be classified as a business and taxed as such—a move which would be an existential threat to the organisation.

Among the many massive hits contained in Natalie Moses' statement of claim, it was easy to miss one telling comment on the organisation's culture. Moses raised the issue of an offensive joke made in her presence by Hillsong's in-house legal counsel, Tim Whincop, which she said had unsettled her 'due to the male-dominated culture at Hillsong, where she did not feel equal to men and was never going to have equal access to opportunities'.

In a May 2022 email to Whincop, Moses said that 'leaders should take accountability when they made a mistake, repent and make a sincere effort to do better'. She then zeroed in on what she said would continue to affect trust among staff: the fact that the board and executive had 'covered up the conduct of [Brian] Houston' and 'never took full accountability for the cover up'. Moses added that 'a cover-up [was] often worse than the crime' and that until 'key people openly apologise and repent to the staff and demonstrate that they understand they made the wrong choices, it was going to be difficult for staff to trust them'.

Hillsong had an answer to that. They denied her claims and decided to fight her in court. The church's actions set off a bruising legal battle that consumed the Moses family financially, emotionally and spiritually. All this occurred at a time when the church was proclaiming publicly that it was cleaning out the stables once and for all, and that a new day of truth had dawned.

As the charities regulator continued its probe, and with Natalie Moses' case against the church brewing, Hillsong decided to retain the heaviest hitter in Australian charities law, the specialist lawyer Murray Baird. He was uniquely placed to do the job. As the ACNC's inaugural assistant commissioner and general counsel in 2012, Baird had helped set up and lead the regulator.

Most potently, he had provided the legal firepower for Word Investments in the landmark charities case decided by the High Court in 2008. That decision—which granted tax-exempt status for charities running profit-making businesses, so long as the profits went to advancing religion—had marked a turning point in the fortunes of Australia's church charities.

Meanwhile, Natalie and Glen Moses became outcasts. Despite the church proclaiming a new era of honesty—a time of no more secrets—Hillsong did what it has always done: closed ranks and pushed the dissidents out into the cold. A rumour circulated that it was Natalie Moses' plan all along to take the job at Hillsong in order to gather information to take the church down.

'There was just all kinds of stupid stuff like that happening,' Glen remembers. 'During this whole time, not one single pastor or anyone from pastoral care or anything reached out to us. I get it, they were taking sides, but I also know that they were instructed not to. We were just actually physically cut off from the church and from any support. Nobody in the church who had a position of power or authority was allowed to speak to us.'

———

The ACNC's investigation, on which Natalie Moses had been working before she finally blew the whistle, wasn't the first time Hillsong had had a problem with regulators.

In the years before the ACNC was created, the NSW Office of Fair Trading had wanted answers from Brian Houston on apparent reporting breaches by a not-for-profit organisation that handled Houston's income from Hillsong and his book-writing and speaking fees on the lucrative Pentecostal preaching circuit. The organisation, Leadership Ministries Inc. (LMI), had received tens of thousands of dollars in so-called 'love offerings' whenever Brian Houston spoke at churches that were not part of Hillsong.

LMI had also purchased two properties from the Houstons. It paid $650,000 for an apartment owned by Bobbie Houston in a block on Bondi Beach in 2002 and also paid Bobbie and Brian $780,000 in 2004 for a property on the Hawkesbury River, north of Sydney. Separately, there were inter-church transfers of $69,041 to LMI for 'contracted services'. The church responded that the properties were used by the Houstons for ministry purposes, 'in a similar way that many churches or ministries would provide a manse for their ministers'.

The New South Wales government investigation escalated into an examination by the Australian Taxation Office (ATO) into LMI. Subsequently, a full-blown tabloid exposé on the

Houstons and their 'lavish tax-free lifestyle' was published in July 2010 in Sydney's *Sunday Telegraph*. Along the way, Brian Houston was forced to put on the public record, via an open letter, what perks he received.

'Hillsong Church has always been about God and People. Every day we hear wonderful stories about how this church is directly impacting the lives of people both here in Australia, and abroad,' the pastor began, before detailing the benefits he and Bobbie received, separate from the property deals. As of 2010, Houston said, his 'total personal income from Hillsong Church in its entirety' was 'just on $150,000 including fringe benefits plus currently the use of a Holden Caprice, along with just over another $150,000 from Leadership Ministries which makes up my complete personal income. If you want to get really personal, I drive a Holden, Bobbie drives a three-year-old Audi Q7, and I ride a motorbike,' he said. (This, of course, was his Harley-Davidson. And the Holden in later years became an Audi.)

Houston claimed the ATO had taken a close look at LMI ('along with many other religious organisations') and had found nothing to worry about. 'Following our professional advice, we have been assured more than once (including by the tax department) that LMI is an appropriate vehicle for the unique ministry that Bobbie and I do, outside the walls of Hillsong Church,' he wrote.

Ever tough under fire, Australia's most senior Pentecostal pastor took up the cudgels against those who would have churches pay tax: 'Undoubtedly, there is a push from some quarters of society to tax churches—which would mean that across the nation; hundreds of millions of dollars that currently goes toward helping people, including the poor, disenfranchised and hurting, would no longer be able to do so,' he said.

Houston's defence of the tax breaks came in the months after the head of the Australian Treasury, Ken Henry, had finalised his major review of Australia's tax system, commissioned by the Rudd government in 2008. The Henry Review found that fringe-benefits tax (FBT) concessions gave charitable organisations a competitive advantage in labour markets, by enabling them to pay the market wage at a lower cost to them. It recommended that the FBT benefits for not-for-profit entities, including religious charities, be phased out and replaced by direct government funding.

Brian Houston said he had 'never personally been a campaigner for fringe benefits (allowances for pastors and charity workers) and though it is clear that it translates into more money being able to go into the good work of ministry; I would not personally be adverse [sic] to the amount of non-taxable fringe benefits being capped at certain income levels'.

But there was no need to worry. The Rudd government made no changes to the FBT exemptions for charities. This was part of a long tradition of government inaction when it comes to religious institutions.

Nor had the official charities investigation, begun in 2022, yielded any serious change. Indeed, Hillsong carried on with business as usual, with its secrets kept hidden and with no public announcements from the ACNC.

Natalie Moses' action against Hillsong was discontinued in 2023 on undisclosed terms. It meant none of the allegations of Hillsong's financial trickery was aired in open court.

However, that was set to change, via a truly spectacular dump of internal Hillsong documents in the federal parliament.

'Fraud, Money Laundering and Tax Evasion'

Precisely twelve months after the shock of Brian Houston's removal from Hillsong, a second explosion rocked the empire.

Shortly after noon on 9 March 2023, an independent member of the federal parliament, Andrew Wilkie, received the speaker's nod and took to his feet in the House of Representatives. Under the rules governing members' statements, Wilkie was allowed five minutes to speak.

As the clock ticked down, Wilkie quickened his delivery to get onto the public record as much as he could of what he knew of Hillsong's inner workings. Skipping over paragraphs to make up time, the Member for Clark, in central Hobart, made quickfire reference to Hillsong's financial affairs, as detailed in a massive trove of documents—some 25,000 in all, and dating back around fifteen years—which he was tabling that day.

Wilkie's statement was made under parliamentary privilege, which meant he could say pretty much whatever he wanted without fear of being sued by Hillsong or any individual. With a practised eye for media exposure, Wilkie would later wheel a trolley-load of documents from the chamber and along the corridors to the tabling office. This would provide a key image for the television news that evening: a volume of internal

Hillsong papers so great that it could only be transported on wheels.

In remarks calculated to generate headlines, Wilkie ran through a list of Hillsong excesses, leading off with allegations that the church had broken 'numerous laws' in Australia and around the world relating to 'fraud, money laundering and tax evasion'. It sounded more like the activities of an organised crime network than a church.

The allegations included:

- That members of the Houston family and their friends had enjoyed a luxury retreat in Cancun, Mexico, using $150,000 of church money while Australia was in strict Covid-19 lockdown;

- That Brian Houston treated private jets 'like Ubers', with trips which cost $55,000, $52,000 and $30,000 in one three-month period;

- That church money donated by parishioners was being used for 'shopping that would embarrass a Kardashian', including a $6500 Cartier watch for Bobbie Houston, $2500 in Louis Vuitton luggage as well as 'shopping sprees for designer clothes at Saks Fifth Avenue'. Add to that 'two watches worth $15,000' for a senior Hillsong pastor and his wife.

- That cash gifts were paid of $15,000 to mark the fiftieth birthday of long-serving Hillsong figure, Darren Kitto, as well as $36,000 to mark 30 years' service of another senior Hillsong pastor, Gary Clarke.

- That 'curious payments' of $10,000 each were made to international pastors Paul de Jong and Chris Hodges, who had investigated allegations of Brian Houston's 2019 misconduct in a Sydney hotel room.

According to Wilkie, 'the criminality' wasn't limited to Australia. He also placed in the spotlight the long-running practice of international pastors being paid tax-free honorariums for speaking at each other's churches—a system which, he said, was used to disguise income and avoid tax.

'For example, US pastor Joyce Meyer enjoyed honorariums of $160,000, $130,000, $100,000 and $32,000,' Wilkie said. 'And US pastor T.D. Jakes got honorariums of $71,000 and $120,000, with a staggering $77,000 worth of airfares to and from Australia thrown in. And, in return, Mr Houston goes to America and received his own eye-watering honorariums.'

Willkie also cited the example of the disgraced former head of the New York Hillsong Church, Carl Lentz, being paid a salary of $220,000 in 2016, 'most of it tax-free, and tens of thousands of dollars in church donations to run the New York church's celebrity "green room" to cover catering and the cost of gifts for visiting celebrities'.

Wilkie's statement landed like a dirty big rock in the Hillsong pond. It is little wonder it took an independent member of parliament to do it. None of the major parties—Labor, Liberal or National—would dare risk alienating religious voters.

———

The revelations generated a series of lurid headlines and a load of outraged commentary. Hillsong itself cried foul. It issued a statement rebutting some of Wilkie's claims—although, notably, it did not seek to defend the departed Houstons:

> Hillsong Church has been open and transparent with our congregation about past governance failures, and over the past 12 months we have engaged independent, professional assistance to overhaul our governance and accountability procedures.
>
> Hillsong is a different church now than we were twelve months ago, and we are under new pastoral and board leadership. We are working hard to set a course for the future that ensures our structures are accountable, transparent, and honouring to God. Anything less has the potential to hinder our primary focus, which is to be a community of believers focused on the life-changing power of Jesus, driven to bring hope to the world around us.

Andrew Wilkie did not identify the source of the internal documents. Hillsong didn't name the person it considered to be the source, but its comments pointed to Natalie Moses:

> The claims made in federal Parliament by Mr Andrew Wilkie are out of context and relate to untested allegations made by an employee in an ongoing legal case. These allegations, made under parliamentary privilege, are in many respects wrong and it is disappointing he made no effort to contact us first. If he did so we would have answered his questions and provided him with financial records to address his concerns.

Hillsong has sought independent legal and accounting advice on these matters since the employee involved in the legal case made these claims, and we believe that we have complied with all legal and compliance requirements . . . We are fully cooperating with regulatory authorities as part of their enquiries.

Hillsong was wounded, angry and feeling misunderstood. Finally, it attempted to turn the narrative from the past to the future. 'Transitions are difficult, uncertain, and sometimes painful,' it concluded. 'However with new leadership, opportunities, and fresh vision we are focused on being a church that loves people and impacts the world.'

By the following Sunday, and with a few days to strategise, the church had hardened its opposition to Wilkie and his use of parliamentary privilege. Board chairman and Hillsong lifer Pastor Stephen Crouch told the congregation that it was difficult not to feel like Wilkie's speech was 'just another attack on our church'. But the Bible—specifically, Jeremiah 33—had the answer.

'But now take another look,' Crouch quoted from the scriptures. 'I'm going to give this city a thorough renovation, working a true healing inside and out. I'm going to show them life, whole life brimming with blessings. I'll restore everything that is lost to Judah and Jerusalem. I'll build everything back as good as new. I'll scrub them clean from the dirt they've done against me.'

Brian Houston's replacement as global senior pastor, Phil Dooley, conceded that the allegations were 'very concerning'.

A 'full forensic investigation' had already been conducted by accounting firm Grant Thornton.

It was 'particularly un-Australian', Dooley continued, for Andrew Wilkie to use parliamentary privilege the way he had. 'It kind of feels like being king-hit from behind,' he said. 'But Jesus loves you, Mr Wilkie.'

The Tax-free Paradise Revealed

How serious was the alleged misuse of church money aired in the Australian parliament? Andrew Wilkie's claims painted a picture of a church very far removed from the traditional version, where the minister might make do with a second-hand Toyota and modest rooms in the presbytery.

Those who attended Hillsong were learning for the first time where their hard-earned donations and tithes were going. The church royalty might have considered that their spending was restrained compared to the excesses of the American televangelists. The biggest of them all, Kenneth Copeland, didn't bother with hiring a private jet here and there: he owned two of them outright. And he kept them at an airfield which he—or his ministry—owned. Other US pastors boasted New York apartments, beachside holiday homes and top-of-the-line luxury cars.

But this was of little comfort to the Hillsong members who had sacrificed so much to support the church's work. If the Houstons thought their spending was not outrageous, then they were totally out of kilter with their congregation.

Important details were hidden in the thousands of documents tabled by Andrew Wilkie. Getting to the bottom of them would take time and some serious digging. It would also reveal exactly how Hillsong had taken maximum advantage of Australia's charities laws, which allow churches to avoid paying tax while all but ensuring they can never be made publicly accountable. Could there be a better business model?

Andrew Wilkie had alleged that Hillsong earned $80 million more in Australian annual income than it reported publicly. How did they do it? And what other secrets did the documents reveal? What had really been happening inside the 'Till on the Hill'?

———

The tabled documents gave further details on the honorarium 'scam', as the whistleblower called it. The extravagant fees for those on the celebrity pastor speaking circuit were ultimately paid for by the tithes and offerings of churchgoers. It is likely, though, that those churchgoers have never known the scale of the fees they have been paying.

The whistleblower made the case that the funds paid to international megachurch pastors who visit Australia—and walk away with tens of thousands of dollars—are derived from tax-exempt charities, which amounts to an abuse of the system.

A lengthy schedule of payments included in the tabled documents showed that Brian Houston was paid to speak at the megachurches of prominent international pastors, many of whom were old friends of the Houstons. The payments add up to more than $1 million in the ten years from 2011.

Prominent among them are US pastors Bill Johnson and his Bethel church in Redding; Casey Treat and his Christian Faith Center in Seattle; Judah Smith and his City Church, also in Seattle; Chris Hodges from Church of the Highlands in Alabama; and Jentezen Franklin and his Free Chapel Church in Georgia.

Houston had also picked up fees for speaking at churches in the far-flung Hillsong empire: Hillsong Cape Town, Hillsong France, Hillsong Germany, Hillsong Los Angeles, Hillsong London, Hillsong Monterrey (Mexico), Hillsong Norway and Hillsong Phoenix.

The documents showed for the first time just how much money was washing through several Hillsong charities that have operated under a cloak of secrecy for years. These are the so-called Basic Religious Charities, which gave Hillsong near blanket exemptions on public disclosure and which are effectively beyond the reach of the Australian regulator.

The documents showed that one charity, the HC Australia Property Trust, held property assets of $68 million. Another, the Trustee for Community Venues, held $23 million in assets.

Notes made by the unnamed whistleblower, which were also tabled in parliament, questioned whether or not these charities met the definition of a Basic Religious Charity [BRC]: 'It is unclear how the [trusts] which exist solely to hold the property of Hillsong can be categorised as Basic Religious Charities by the ACNC (which regulates Australia's charities), thus allowing them to "hide" their financials from both the ACNC and the public,' the whistleblower concluded.

A third charity, the Trustee for Hillsong International—the music and resources arm of Hillsong in Australia—had total income of $42 million in its 2021 accounts, and held assets valued at $29 million. Its main source of income was $12 million in royalties on Hillsong music. It also received 'donations' of $11 million, all coming from other Hillsong-related entities and affiliated churches.

The whistleblower asked the thorny question of whether this charity should in fact be classified as a business, and therefore be taxed:

> If the only 'donations' Hillsong International receives are from other Hillsong-related entities, it receives no donations from the general public, and its commercials (commercial earnings) are material, it is possible [the charity] should be classified as a business. At the very least Hillsong International could be considered ineligible to be registered as a BRC with the ACNC.

Whatever the answer, moving money around at will from one Hillsong charity to another, it could be argued, made a mockery of the idea of an individual Hillsong charity having its own distinct mission.

The Trustee for Hillsong International encompasses a dozen separate entities, which drive the music and broadcast operations. It was eligible for tax breaks because, according to its trust deed, its purpose is to 'advance the Christian faith of Hillsong church and its global ministries in Australia' in accordance with its statement of belief—an eleven-point document which includes that 'the Holy Spirit enables us to use spiritual gifts, including speaking in tongues'. Of all the eye-popping anomalies about Hillsong's tax breaks, this one probably takes the cake.

A number of operations housed within the charity were linked directly to members of the Houston family. TSGTV, The Secret Garden Television, was a web-based broadcasting venture set up by the Houstons' daughter, Laura, as an avenue for talking about spiritual nourishment with young women. The Colour Sisterhood was Bobbie Houston's personal venture, creating an annual conference for Hillsong women.

Hillsong United was one of the first music groups to come out of Hillsong. It's led by Bobbie and Brian's son Joel, who has been a central player in the fortune-generating industry of Hillsong music. He also has his own charity registered in Australia, called Parable Ministries, which is eligible for a range of tax breaks. On top of that, he is a pastor and therefore eligible for tax dispensations that go with that.

Brian Houston was credited as the executive producer of albums made by the long-running Hillsong music group called Hillsong Worship, many of which went gold or platinum on the American worship music charts, generating massive income.

Hillsong music also comes in other guises that aren't immediately recognisable. Under the brand name City and Vine Music Publishing, the church sells licences and manages copyright for Hillsong compositions and performances. Hillsong music is used by other churches, but it has also been used in television advertisements for Mercedes-Benz, Nike, PlayStation and Under Armour.

How the enormous income generated by Hillsong music is distributed has always caused friction. The cache of parliamentary documents revealed the huge sums of money sloshing around. One document covering payments to Hillsong's high earners in 2021 showed that a small group of celebrity songwriters—who are virtually unknown outside the Christian music scene—had been paid a small fortune.

Worship director Brooke Ligertwood, a leading singer-songwriter, had received $1.7 million, with the majority of that being $1.5 million in royalties. Music pastor Ben Fielding was paid over $1.5 million, with $1.4 million of that being royalties from Hillsong music sales. Another music pastor, Matthew Crocker, made over $800,000.

The Houstons, naturally, were high on the list. Joel Houston, titled as Global Creative Director, earned $1.9 million (not including book royalties or bonuses for music tours). Brian Houston was paid at least $1 million that year, with royalties and book sales not disclosed. Bobbie Houston was paid nearly $500,000, with royalties not disclosed.

———

Another aspect of Hillsong which the Wilkie documents detailed for the first time was the international franchise model, which delivers numbers and wealth to the church's head office.

As described earlier, the franchise model is a two-tiered system made up of churches owned and operated by Hillsong and so-called 'Hillsong Family Churches', which have a degree of autonomy from the Hillsong mothership.

According to the Hillsong whistleblower's disclosures, the wholly owned churches send 5 per cent of their income as a tithe to Hillsong HQ.

In Australia, the total tithe income to the church was around $48 million in 2021, and $52 million in 2020. This was down marginally on the $56 million in 2019, the year before Covid-19 put a halt to church gatherings.

The 40 Hillsong Family Churches around the world pass on 3 per cent of their tithe income as 'membership fees' to Hillsong; the amount is capped at $100,000 per church. Under the arrangement, the smaller church keeps its name and is able to use Hillsong 'branding'.

As noted earlier, one of the attractions of the 'Family Church' pay-to-play model is that pastors from small churches can network at the 'exclusive' Hillsong Family Gathering held twice a year at an overseas location.

Underpinning all this was a corporate structure that delivered control over the Hillsong empire to a handful of people clustered around Brian Houston. Although there were dozens of different Hillsong entities in Australia and overseas, the same names come up again and again on the Hillsong boards which governed each entity (most of them charities).

Leading the pack, Global Senior Pastor Brian Houston was listed as a director on 31 different corporate entities. His son Ben sat on more than twenty Hillsong boards. Darren Kitto, a senior and trusted Hillsong figure, was a director on twenty boards, mainly of overseas entities.

The Wilkie documents contained a 30-page listing of the interlocking interests of the Hillsong directors and entities, underlining what the whistleblower said were the conflicts of interest among Hillsong's board of directors when making decisions. 'This structure enables a core group of Directors to have significant power, control and influence over all Hillsong operations globally,' the whistleblower concluded. 'This level of power and control enabled the significant private benefit enjoyed by Brian and Bobbie Houston during their reign at Hillsong.'

Separate to that, records showed that, each year, the boards of Hillsong Global and Hillsong Australia would sign resolutions stating that they would not call upon any intercompany loans for the next twelve months and one day, thus creating a perpetual rollover of 'loans'. This, the whistleblower concluded, is 'how Hillsong launders money throughout its different entities in Australia and overseas'.

———

One interested observer of the Hillsong corporate phenomenon has been Ted Sherwood, a certified practising accountant who has kept a close watch on religious charities through his website called 'Business by the Book'. Sherwood provides independent reviews of Christian charities, which donors can check before deciding where to put their money. Through his work he has also become something of a thorn in the side of the ACNC.

Sherwood analysed Hillsong's public filings on its nineteen Australian charities, as they stood when Brian Houston ruled the roost. He found that nearly all had a direct ownership link back to Hillsong's US company, Hillsong USA Inc., which is registered in Texas. In eleven cases, the senior pastor of the US entity was, according to the constitution of that charity, an ex-officio director. In ten of those cases it was a lifetime appointment. At the date the entities were registered, the senior pastor was Brian Houston.

From Hillsong's admittedly limited public disclosures, Sherwood was nevertheless able to discern that intercompany loans and transactions were 'common'. He independently identified an extreme concentration of power in the governance of the charities, with just seven individuals controlling 113 of the 121 board positions across all the charities.

Except for just two directors, Hillsong directors each sat on at least fifteen boards at the time of his checking. This raises the question of how they could possibly do justice to their duties as a director of an individual charity. As a rule of thumb in the corporate world, when an individual is on more than four to five directorships, they are considered to be 'overboarded'.

Ultimately, Sherwood found, the corporate arrangement placed power in one person above all—the senior pastor—giving him near unquestioned authority.

Too Big to Fail

The Houstons and Hillsong came undone because their secrets caught up with them. Their extraordinary rise, though, was enabled in large part by Australia's federal government, which enabled the creation of the Hillsong business model and then permitted it to operate with minimal interference. Hillsong then became untouchable in the eyes of successive governments, whose leaders were desperate for the faith vote and the aspirational vote—or both, in the case of Hillsong.

Hillsong employee Natalie Moses' revelations on the church's financial dealings told another story, too: that Australia's charities regulator, the ACNC, had been incapable of regulating a complex multinational operation like Hillsong.

Really, Hillsong should be grateful. The years of official inaction covered the precise period of the church's greatest growth, which was fuelled by the tax-free millions sloshing into, through and around the myriad Hillsong charities run under various corporate names, as well as separate charities operated by Hillsong pastors and board members.

The ACNC is one of those government bodies that flies under the radar. Most Australians have very little, if anything, to do with it. There might be the occasional news item about a charity rip-off being exposed, but that's generally it. But the ACNC is part of the Canberra bureaucracy. It is linked to the Australian Taxation Office, because charities are eligible for exemptions from paying federal taxes such as the GST, fringe-benefits tax and income tax.

As a relative of the ATO, you might think the ACNC is an organisation to be feared—that it would come down hard on any charity organisation that fiddles its books or misuses public donations. Nothing could be further from the truth—especially if your charity is a large and complex one, and especially if it has a religious purpose. Hillsong fits that bill, but so too do the traditional religious denominations, with their various trusts and benevolent operations.

If the charity sector can be said to belong to any one interest group, then it is the churches. The most recent ACNC data shows that 30 per cent of Australia's 46,500 charities describe themselves as having a religious purpose. Next comes those involved in primary and secondary education (9 per cent) and 'other education' (8 per cent).

Of the 15,000 or so charities with a religious purpose, around 8400—more than half—claim they are in the subcategory known as a Basic Religious Charity. As such, they are virtually beyond the reach of the regulator. Under the ACNC's establishment legislation, a Basic Religious Charity doesn't need to provide any financial information to the regulator. Nor can the regulator remove an office holder.

In other words, there are 8400 religious charities that are effectively a law unto themselves.

So what are the chances of a religious organisation being caught out by the charity regulator? Bearing in mind the ACNC's investigation record, the answer is: virtually nil. The agency's latest records show that, in a twelve-month period, only 96 investigations were completed into complaints made about Australia's charities. A grand total of fifteen had their charity status revoked.

There's another protection built into the ACNC design: by law, the regulator cannot comment publicly on individual charity cases, no matter how much it would be in the public interest to do so. Media questions about potential wrongdoing therefore go unanswered.

Ted Sherwood, the accountant who keeps an eye on the public filings by religious charities with the ACNC, has created a list of the ways the regulator fails to do its job or has been nobbled by successive governments. He cites around a dozen administrative pitfalls, which have the effect of allowing a charity to keep key data off the public record for months or years at a time without consequence. When it comes to compliance, he says, the regulator simply lacks the staff to be effective.

Sherwood points to one striking statistic: no director of a charity has been struck off in the ACNC's decade of operation.

Australia's churches have powerful lobby groups that work to maintain the political status quo. The major umbrella organisation representing the not-for-profit sector includes two high-profile church figures on its board. One is the Reverend Tim Costello, the well-known Baptist minister and former CEO of one of Australia's largest Christian charities, World Vision. The other is Hillsong's general manager, and long-term friend and defender of the Houston family, George Aghajanian.

In the view of charity and taxation law specialists, there has never been any sound policy basis for the Basic Religious Charity dispensation. It was an exemption made for reasons of political expediency in 2012, when the Gillard government's Australian Charities and Not-for-Profits Commission Bill was having difficulty passing the Senate, and was under intense religious lobbying, led by the Catholic Archdiocese of Sydney and its archbishop, Cardinal George Pell. Pell reputedly said he would not put up with 'the state' putting its hand into his church's collection plate. Hillsong was a clear beneficiary of Pell's assertion of power.

The best chance to right this policy wrong came in 2018, when the Turnbull government held a review into the ACNC's operations. One of the most powerful arguments to end the secrecy provision that applied to Basic Religious Charities stemmed from the work of the Royal Commission into Institutional Responses to Child Sexual Abuse. One of the six commissioners, Robert Fitzgerald, said the royal commission had demonstrated a need for 'greater transparency and accountability in relation to all non-profits, but particularly charitable organisations'.

Fitzgerald was uniquely qualified to offer a view. A former Productivity Commissioner, he was chair of the ACNC's advisory board when it was established in 2012. Fitzgerald had also served on the boards of Catholic charitable organisations, such as Caritas Australia, so he could hardly be accused of being anti-religious. Fitzgerald articulated his reasoning in an address he gave in early 2018:

How is it possible that so many not-for-profit organisations who talk about justice, integrity and truth abandoned all of those values so quickly when adults came forward to disclose the abuse that had happened to them, as children, in the royal commission? For me, for the whole five years of the royal commission, that was the question.

The answer became clearer and clearer as we went on. And that was that the three elements that are essential to the good functioning of an organisation—governance, leadership and culture—were failing.

How do we change institutions that have been so trusted by the Australian community into safer, healthier places, not only for children, but for all those that come to those institutions with vulnerabilities? That is the challenge that we now face. It's not just about child sexual abuse. It's really about how we govern for the vulnerable.

I think the challenge here really is very significant: that organisations that were found wanting in the royal commission cannot stand in the marketplace of values without also embracing fully and wholeheartedly the value of transparency and accountability. It is inconsistent.

Fitzgerald's address provided an all but irrefutable case to change the rules for religious charities. The heads of secular charitable organisations also called for greater transparency across religious charities to ensure greater public trust and confidence.

Ultimately, the federal government chose to ignore the evidence, even as it offered apologies and compensation for the behaviour of religious organisations, as revealed by the royal commission.

The federal government's review into the ACNC was tabled to parliament in August 2018. It landed just as Scott Morrison was taking over as prime minister from Malcolm Turnbull.

It was eighteen months before, finally, in 2020, the Morrison government responded. On the question of the Basic Religious

Charity, it provided a single-line answer to the detailed, evidence-based case against the secretive charities: 'The government has no plans to review the exemptions for Basic Religious Charities.' End of story.

9
THE RAPTURE

Pastor Scott

Brian Houston came unstuck in March 2022. Two months later, in May, it was the turn of Scott Morrison, along with the Liberal Party he had fashioned in his image. It too came unstuck largely because of its secrecy and its hostility to accountability—indeed, to any process of transparent government.

The rise and fall of Brian Houston and Hillsong has been accompanied, in many respects, by the rise and fall of Scott Morrison and his wing of the Liberal Party. Both have left a legacy that must be reckoned with.

When Morrison lost power in 2022, his first public act was to present himself to his local Pentecostal church, where he found solace in Biblical verses about withered vines and trees that had ceased to fruit.

His next public act was to travel to the Victory Life Centre in Perth—the Pentecostal church of former tennis great Margaret Court—where he sermonised on the supremacy of God over government.

He also accepted an invitation from his 'dear friend' Mike Pompeo, the former US Secretary of State and a fellow Pentecostal Christian, to join him on the board of the China Center, attached to a neoconservative Washington think tank called the Hudson Institute.

In all three settings, Morrison was finally among friends. And in his sermon at Margaret Court's church, he was ready at last to give the finger to his enemies in the secular world and declare fully his motivation.

Morrison had been invited to a special service to commemorate the completion of a new prayer tower next to the Victory Life Centre. The soaring landmark was the dream of Margaret Court, who had recently received her promotion to Companion of the Order of Australia (AC), the highest position in the Australian honours list.

He arrived without a care as to any blowback that might come his way for linking hands with Court, a polarising figure whose views on homosexuality had marginalised her in the world of tennis and beyond. All that prime ministerial concern with voter backlash concerning his traditional views was well behind him.

Morrison presented a 50-minute sermon that rivalled anything a seasoned Pentecostal pastor might produce. Indeed, the sermon could have been the work of Brian Houston himself.

That shouldn't be surprising, really, as Morrison had been steeped in the Bible for four decades, ever since he embraced God as a twelve-year-old attending a Christian Boys' Brigade camp.

At the Victory Life Centre, he was more than happy to promote his Christian pedigree, including that he had spent years in the hardcore evangelical movement known as the Christian Brethren—a part of his background which he had kept obscured for most of his time in public life.

The headline for the watching media that day was Morrison's attack on the very system of government over which he had presided for more than three years, and which had given him a platform in public life for well over a decade. In so doing, he made it crystal clear to the world that secular government wasn't to be trusted. He called on worshippers to put their faith in religion instead. For good measure, Morrison also took a swipe at the United Nations, which is disdained by some fundamentalists as a secular threat to the one-world government of God. This belief is known as dominion theology, the name alluding to Adam having 'dominion over every creature' in the Garden of Eden.

'God's kingdom will come,' he pronounced. 'It's in his hands. We trust in him. We don't trust in governments. We don't trust in the United Nations, thank goodness. We don't trust in all these things, fine as they may be and as important as the role that they play. Believe me, I've worked in it and they are important. But as someone who's been in it, if you are putting your faith in those things as I put my faith in the Lord, you're making a mistake. They are earthly, they are fallible. I'm so glad we have a bigger hope.'

Morrison had said such things before—notably, a year earlier at the Pentecostal church conference—but no one in the political commentariat had paid much attention.

As prime minister, Morrison had lashed the UN, going so far as to order the Department of Foreign Affairs and Trade to undertake a 'comprehensive audit' of global institutions and rule-making processes. At that time, he drew on the 'negative globalism' sentiment coming from the Trump administration, rather than placing it in a religious context, as he was doing now.

The former prime minister's theme for the day was the epidemic of mental health problems in Australia. At the core of the mental health crisis, he said, was anxiety. 'It's shaking our nation,' he told his congregation, pointing to 'the droughts and the floods and the fires and the pandemics', including even a mouse plague in New South Wales. The world, too, was engulfed in troubled times, with war in Ukraine and instability in the Indo-Pacific (former Japanese prime minister Shinzo Abe had recently been assassinated). Young people were anxious about the climate, the environment and the future of the world.

If the world was going to hell and anxiety had gripped the land, then the former PM had the answer: accept the power and grace of God. 'Be anxious for nothing,' was his reassurance and his providential promise. Morrison had moved anxiety from being a psychological issue to a spiritual issue. In this framework, God is the healer, and an individual's belief in God is the pathway to healing—because God knows you better than you know yourself.

In a sense, there is nothing exceptional about the idea that religion is a balm for worldly cares. But what was exceptional was where Morrison took the idea next.

'When I look carefully at the many treatments that [are] provided, particularly for people dealing with anxiety, I see a lot of parallels about what I had always known about God, and how God seeks to engage with us,' he said. 'It's funny how that happens, isn't it? That people in a secular sphere discover what we already know in a spiritual sphere.'

Morrison was now enunciating a common Christian view: that all the knowledge we need already exists in the Bible, and science is simply catching up. This view also applies to issues such as climate science.

Morrison developed his theme of anxiety to take in the topic of identity politics, a culture war issue that had been prominent during his prime ministership. How Morrison managed to spiritualise this issue was especially illuminating:

'Who are you? It's called identity politics, and something I've always railed against: this idea that you're defined by your gender or your sexuality or whatever it happens to be, that this is who you are. Defined by your race, your background, what language you speak.

'No. You're defined as an individual, amazing creation of God. Each and every single human being is unique. And we need to respect that you're not defined by your grievance or your offence or being part of some collective set of grievances to which you have to constantly assert out there. You're not defined by that; you're defined by who you are uniquely, individually as a human being.

'And guess what the most defining characteristic of that is? That God loves you. You're worried about who you are? There's one answer: God loves you. You're worried about your identity? You are completely embraced in those three words. God. Loves. You. For who you are.'

How did Morrison's audience of evangelical Christians receive his message? It takes someone who has sat through years of such sermons to understand how a Pentecostal ear hears what's being said.

The phrase 'we're all one in Christ' represents a theology that calls for unity and harmony in the body of Christ amid all that divides humans. As such, argues Cara Phillips—who was raised on the scriptures in an evangelical home before becoming a whistleblower on institutional religious abuses— it negates the secular view that inequality is systemic, suggesting instead that simply being in Christ is enough to make everyone equal.

'In public policy terms, the implication is that there is no need to actually help people like asylum seekers, because their real issue isn't that they are seeking asylum. It's that they need Jesus,' Phillips explains. 'Nor do you need to fight for marriage equality—you just need Jesus. You don't need to consider a treaty. If all the Indigenous people just accepted Jesus, they would realise that's all they need. Then they'd be glad they were colonised because we brought Jesus to them.'

Morrison's sermon also provided an answer for those who had wondered at his ability to change his story—to tell lies, really—and then move on as though nothing had happened.

It all lies in God's forgiveness, which, as Morrison himself pointed out, can apply instantly.

'God has forgiven you,' he preached. 'Everything, including the thing you just thought about . . . and whatever those things that you think are holding you back, and the things in your past. And, you know, Satan is known as the accuser, the great accuser, and he'll keep throwing this stuff at you. But God on the cross said, "No, you are forgiven for all of it." Everything, everything you have done, everything that you will do. And so if you're anxious about these things, and these things are holding you down, and they're crushing you down, declare the name of Jesus and declare His forgiveness.'

According to Cara Phillips, who has heard her share of Satan references over the years, Morrison was now talking directly about spiritual warfare.

'The call to declare the name of Jesus was a distinctive Pentecostal touch,' she says. 'It means casting out Satan in the name of Jesus. This marked Morrison not just as "one of us Christians" but as "one of us Pentecostals", because other denominations don't do spiritual warfare. Nor do they really know how to pray, according to Pentecostals.'

Morrison was also promoting the idea that you will suffer and you will not be healed if you don't have enough faith. This was a common strand in Pentecostal preaching. Indeed, the great Frank Houston himself told his congregations in New Zealand that if they weren't healed of their illness, it wasn't God's fault, it was because they didn't truly trust in God. That was back in the 1970s. Thus, the former prime minister came full circle on

50 years of Pentecostal belief, and the direct influence of the Houston family.

Like Frank the prophet and countless other pastors, Morrison completed his sermon with a Sinner's Prayer, also known as a Salvation Prayer. Having marinated his congregation in the balm of the Lord, the former marketing man moved to close the deal. All those who agreed that they were suffering from the ravages of anxiety—and, let's face it, who hasn't?—were asked to 'shoot up' their hand and wait for someone from the church to see them later.

'Heavenly Father,' Pastor Scott began in prayer, then he paused and enjoined the congregation to 'say it with me'. 'Lord Jesus, I acknowledge you as Lord and Saviour. I thank you for sending your son to die for me on that cross to be your price for my sin. Lord, come into my life now. I declare you as my Lord and my saviour. Lord, I invite your Holy Spirit to come and live within me. In Jesus' name. Amen.'

The entire sermon could have been delivered from the stage of a Hillsong mega-gathering.

The more time passed, the more the former prime minister revealed his true colours. In September 2023 a pastor at Perth's Endeavour Christian Gathering church introduced Morrison to the stage with a story which compared Morrison to Jesus, based on the divine properties of the number 30.

'Jesus entered into ministry at thirty; it's a coming-of-age time, And you . . . were not an accident to be the thirtieth Prime Minister of Australia. We needed that,' the pastor said, under-lining the role of a greater power.

Morrison didn't quibble.

'I didn't know that about thirty,' he confessed. 'But now, when you say it, and particularly in terms of when Jesus' ministry started . . . I . . . I . . . Yes, that's true,' he said.

'God has a way of saying things into your life about some of these events.'

This was a cue for Morrison to tell his story of God's intervention in the birth of the Morrison's first child on the seventh day of the seventh month, 2007.

That, again, was proof that God always had a way of reminding us of who's in charge.

'It's not us,' he added. 'And thank God for that.'

With the prime ministership now well in the rear-vision mirror, Morrison spoke with affection of his early days with the Christian Brethren church, which as prime minister he had barely mentioned publicly. Now he was sharing a joke with his evangelical followers about 'the brethos' as he called them, and their habit of plonking a hat on the heads of followers as they arrived for prayers.

The Christian Brethren might be a fringe denomination but they have grown wealthy on property investments buttressed by the generous tax breaks they receive as a church.

On that day in Perth the former prime minister warmed to his role as pastor for a day. He told a story from the Bible about how God intervened to protect the Israelites as they came under attack from the Philistines.

The story, as Morrison portrayed it, contained the lesson that those who sought the Lord would automatically be attacked.

'The minute you decide you are going to get serious about returning to the Lord, coming to the Lord, serving the Lord, the enemy will be on the march straight away,' Morrison said.

Morrison had been reminded of this story of the enemy coming for God's people by 'a really great Christian pastor friend, when I was PM', as he told his audience, without declaring whether or not that might have been Hillsong supremo Brian Houston.

The Pentecostal PM

Scott Morrison had ticked a mighty big box in the Seven Mountains mandate, promoted so assiduously by his close friend and mentor Pastor Brian Houston. His elevation to the prime ministership was a sign of how deeply Pentecostalism had become embedded in the Liberal Party and its conservative, neoliberal base.

Back in 1983, when Brian and Bobbie Houston began their church in the Hills District, Pentecostalism had zero political influence. Over a period of 40 years, it had travelled from the fringes to the mainstream of politics, and then to the epicentre of political power. It did so by colonising the Liberal Party.

Scott Morrison was the steward, but others came in his wake. Fellow Pentecostal Christian Stuart Robert, from the Gold Coast, was a member of Morrison's cabinet. Ben Morton, a key Pentecostal influence in the Western Australia branch of the Liberal Party, became Morrison's Minister for the Public Service, a 'fixer' role which put him in charge of the government instrumentalities of accountability such as the Australian National Audit Office.

Another Western Australian MP, Ian Goodenough, owed his position to a local branch membership dominated by Pentecostal church members. Western Australian senator and fellow Pentecostal Christian Matt O'Sullivan was a prominent player in the cross-party Parliamentary Christian Fellowship.

In Victoria and South Australia, the Liberal Party was engulfed by internal wars over the influence of conservative Christians, largely from Pentecostal church communities. Prior to the 2022 election, Morrison backed Jemima Gleeson, a worship leader with the Hope Unlimited Church, as the party's candidate for a seat in New South Wales. So brazen was the takeover that, in the end, Senator James McGrath publicly accused Morrison of attempting to turn the New South Wales Liberal Party into a branch of Hillsong.

Throughout all these efforts, Brian Houston was Scott Morrison's inspiration, and Hillsong was his light on the hill.

If anything, Pentecostal believers came to be over-represented in the Liberal Party—a sign of how assiduously the church had pumped up its follower base. But the party itself was open for the business of a neoliberal religious brand that had the acquisition of wealth at its core and an entrepreneurial, pay-to-play approach.

In the United States, which became Brian Houston's home base for close to a decade, it was possible, under the right conditions, to engineer fundamental and far-reaching social change with the right agent in the White House. The opportunistic Donald Trump was the man to do that, in exchange for the white evangelical vote. The Republican Party was the natural political host for a neoliberal religious group.

Australia does not have the same religious make-up as the United States. Nor is Australia's government as susceptible to a religious takeover. Nevertheless, Scott Morrison gave it an almighty shake. As prime minister he was in prime position to put into practice Houston's Seven Mountains mandate, his much-trumpeted attempt to exert influence over what Christians regard as the seven pillars of society.

Those who follow '7M', as it is affectionately known, believe that, before Christ can return, the church must take control of these seven spheres. Once the world has been made subject to the kingdom of God, Christ will return and rule the world. That's how vital it is to get control.

———

It's not every day a religious leader seeking to remake government in God's image has a prime minister in his pocket and on speed dial. So what did the Member for Hillsong, Scott Morrison, actually do with all that prime ministerial power?

When it came to saving troubled souls, Morrison put his money—or, more accurately, taxpayers' money—where his faith was. In the weeks before the 2019 election, Morrison promised $4 million to the Esther Foundation, a Pentecostal rehab facility for women and girls suffering emotional and psychological issues, including anxiety, depression, eating disorders, and drug and alcohol addiction.

He made a personal visit to the facility in Perth, and when there he took personal credit for the taxpayer-funded grant, telling staff and residents he didn't 'invest in things that don't work'. The grant was fast-tracked through the government's Department of Health bureaucracy, with scant evidence of any due diligence being performed.

Morrison trumpeted the government's support for this Pentecostal facility during his speech to launch the Liberal Party's 2019 campaign. He called the Esther Foundation 'an amazing organisation'.

It later emerged that the Esther Foundation had for decades used extreme, religious-based practices to 'treat' residents. These included 'pray the gay away' gay conversion therapy, exorcisms and all-night prayer meetings. Girls and young women with clinical conditions were denied prescription medications. As well as emotional and physical abuse, some former residents alleged that they were sexually abused as minors, and that this abuse was kept from the authorities. Allegations of abuse covered a period of more than two decades, while the 'pastor' running the centre claimed she was being directed by God.

In bestowing on the foundation his personal and prime ministerial imprimatur, Morrison gave it an aura of untouchability. He also enhanced his standing no end in the Pentecostal world.

The Esther Foundation's practices replicated the religious-based practices of Mercy Ministries, the Hillsong rehab centre for women and girls which had been forced to close a decade earlier because of media revelations of serious systemic abuse.

Within three years, the Esther Foundation was forced to close down after a series of revelations by online news site *Crikey*. The Western Australian parliament conducted an inquiry into the two decades of abuse at the centre, and ultimately passed laws to make gay conversion therapy illegal.

The Esther Foundation's work had been widely supported by Perth's Pentecostal churches, including Margaret Court's Victory Life Centre. It aligned with Morrison's long-held belief that Christian organisations should be in the business of running rehabilitation services.

Despite the problems with the Mercy Ministries and the Esther Foundation, the idea that faith in God is the cure for psychological and psychiatric problems has proved remarkably resilient within Hillsong and in other Pentecostal and evangelical settings. It remains potent in small evangelical churches, and in the privacy of evangelical homes around the country. And while Hillsong publicly walked away from Mercy Ministries in 2009, it has continued to promote the same approach overseas, where there is less media scrutiny.

In Lima, Peru, Hillsong works in partnership with a church called Camino de Vida ('Path of Life') in a venture called Casa Gracia ('Grace House'). Case Gracia promotes itself as a joint ministry with Hillsong Church 'born out of the desire to retrieve, through the Word of God, everything that the devil has stolen from girls suffering from eating disorders, depression, and a variety of different addictions'.

'Casa Gracia is not a clinic,' it claims, 'but rather a Christian refuge home that provides these girls with the tools they need to fight everyday battles. Overall, it is a place where they will learn about the unconditional love God has for them and the healing that can be found in His unending mercy and grace.'

Hillsong has also kept faith with the idea of God curing behavioural and psychiatric problems when it comes to men's rehabilitation. Alongside Mercy Ministries, Hillsong has been a major supporter of One80TC. 'One80' refers to turning a life around 180 degrees, while the initials 'TC' refer to Teen Challenge, a global faith-based organisation founded by a Pentecostal pastor in the US.

One80TC defines its rehab work as a 'ministry' operating 'in sympathy with the aims and objectives' of the Assemblies of God in Australia—the former name for the umbrella organisation of Australia's Pentecostal churches—and of Teen Challenge worldwide. Its primary long-term objective is to encourage those who have gone through One80TC to engage in further theological studies and remain connected to a local Christian church.

Church attendance is compulsory during the week and on Sundays. Church attendance means Hillsong. And that's exactly where 33-year-old Jacob Harrison found himself, like a fish out of water, having entered One80TC's rehab facility in bushland on Sydney's north-western fringe. Jacob Harrison was an alcohol addict. He needed to kick it somehow, and someone he knew recommended One80TC.

'I came to One80TC direct from a psych ward—a gay man with a working knowledge of Christianity garnered from *Monty Python*,' he says. 'One of my first Sundays at Hillsong, the subject of the sermon happened to be the power of speaking in tongues. I thought it was going to be a lecture. But no, it was the real thing, and we were all going to do it now.

'This was a really frightening experience. The Hillsong campus is huge and all those people putting their hands up and shouting in the air. It's pretty confronting for someone that's, well, just fragile in general and very new to all this.'

Harrison quickly learnt that the best way to cope was to blend in. 'I started reading the Bible and having discussions about it and stuff. And I was putting my hands up and waving them around like I just didn't care. The more you do that, the more you show an interest, the more little freedoms and little things they let you get away with.'

Secular books were banned. Instead, Harrison was left to read religious tracts such as *How to Prophesy*, which he believes had been passed to the facility from Hillsong College. According to Harrison, the 'therapy' took the form of staff members having 'kind of thought bubbles', which they shared.

'That's how Pentecostalism works. You and I might have a thought bubble come into our head and go, "Hmmm, that's interesting. I might write that down." They'll think it's divine intervention, that "God has put this thought in my head, I must share it." It's like the rules of magic apply.'

Ultimately, what Harrison calls the 24/7 bombardment of religion upended his own sense of reality, with disturbing consequences.

'The music of Hillsong is mostly all that you're hearing,' he recalls. 'You also heard people's clearly psychiatric illnesses being described as possible messages from God. This came from One80TC employees who should have recognised that people needed psychiatric care or some kind of higher level of care.

But instead they were validating these voices people were hearing as being messages from God.

'I'd been cut off from my own tribe. The magical thinking had started to make me question my own beliefs, and my own sense of reality. And when that happened, that's what freaked me out.'

Jacob Harrison made good his escape after six months. He completed his rehab in a secular facility, where, he says, there were inspection visits from outsiders.

He has two abiding memories of his time at One80TC. One is being part of the group of One80TC residents taken to Hillsong services and corralled in a corner like exhibits on public display, examples of the Lord's fallen being saved by the godly. Another is the day he found himself washing Brian Houston's car as a 'volunteer' worker at Hillsong's glitzy annual conference. It was hardly the kind of therapy Harrison had in mind.

'You get there at six in the morning and you're working like a dog all day,' he says. 'The international guests that were coming in had sparkly cars. I had to pay special attention to Brian Houston's Audi; I had to clean that inside and out.'

Hillsong describes One80TC as a 'Christ-centred organisation' that is 'more than just a drug and alcohol rehabilitation program'. Harrison thinks of it as a Hillsong induction facility with a mild interest in rehabilitation.

In its own way, Hillsong itself backs Harrison's assessment. In a report to its donors, Hillsong was able to boast that One80TC had produced '80 salvations and 37 baptisms' in the first half of

2022 alone, with eight former One80TC 'students' choosing to stay on for a graduate program, where they volunteer with the 'ministry' for twelve months. It's a measure of success based literally on how many rehab residents seek salvation and open their heart and life to Jesus.

Hillsong has donated large amounts of congregants' money to One80TC. So did the Morrison government, which overturned a Health Department decision to cease its funding. Then it stumped up close to $2 million of public money for the organisation in 2019, at a time when his government appeared likely to be about to be booted out.

The Morrison government's funding of Pentecostal-based 'treatments' slipped under the radar as relatively small items in a federal budget of billions of dollars. They largely escaped media attention.

The case of the Esther Foundation, personally promised $4 million by Morrison, was finally investigated by the Australian National Audit Office (ANAO) more than three years after the Morrison government approved the grant via a fast-tracked process.

The ANAO audit found the grant was approved before (and despite) the Australian Government Solicitor's office warning that the grant would likely be without lawful authority. It confirmed that the federal Health Department had not done necessary financial checks and that the Pentecostal facility was funded for expenses not covered by grant guidelines.

In other words, the Morrison government had completely ignored the processes of good governance.

The ANAO's findings were made public in June 2023, by which stage Morrison was well out of government. The ANAO's judgement was savage but as a form of accountability, it came late and meant little.

Morrison's work as a Pentecostal standard bearer in government was done. It made him a hero to the movement without him suffering a single consequence.

At the same time the then PM's public seal of approval for Esther acted as the ultimate deterrence for any young woman who might speak up about the facility.

Preparing for the End of Days

Commentators largely dismissed the idea that Scott Morrison's Christianity influenced his actions in government. How could a Christian enforce a cruel asylum-seeker policy that saw children held in offshore detention? How could a Christian support the 'robodebt' scheme of recouping alleged overpayments of government benefits in a way that inflicted pain on the most vulnerable?

The real question is not whether or not Morrison acted like a Christian in government. It is whether or not his actions were influenced by the model of Pentecostal Christianity promoted by Brian Houston and Hillsong. In some ways, Houston's brand of prosperity Pentecostalism is so perfectly intertwined with neoliberal thinking that it is difficult to say where the religion stops and the political policy begins.

Morrison's prime ministership is littered with examples, small and large, of his Hillsong-style practice. Apart from his support for evangelical rehab clinics, the Esther Foundation and

One80TC, many examples have gone unreported, or have been misunderstood by reporters who have not grasped the significance of religion.

A clear instance was Morrison's push for Australia to recognise the holy city of Jerusalem as the capital of Israel, rather than Tel Aviv, which aligned him with Donald Trump's secretary of state, Mike Pompeo, another fervent Pentecostal believer occupying high office.

Morrison tried hard, meanwhile, to deliver on his promise of a religious discrimination bill before the 2022 election. The bill promised to make discrimination on the ground of religious belief or activity unlawful in certain areas of public life, including employment, and was aimed at answering the concerns of faith groups after the passing of laws legalising same-sex marriage. The debate raised hot-button gender and identity issues, and played into the never-ending culture war waged by the Murdoch media. Ultimately, Morrison's legislation split his own party, with so-called moderate Liberal members of parliament threatening to cross the floor and vote against Morrison, who enforced marathon sittings of parliament over an issue that seemed peripheral to most voters. Subsequently, Morrison backed the highly controversial 'values' candidate Katherine Deves, whose sole policy position appeared to be to oppose participation by transgender competitors in women's sport.

Even as political observers demanded to know which government policies bore the stamp of Morrison's religious beliefs, they missed the most striking piece of evidence. Indeed, the defining characteristic of Morrison's prime ministership was his antipathy towards the idea of secular accountability, which most Australians see as key to the functioning of our democracy.

Morrison's attack on process and accountability was unprecedented in Liberal Party tradition. But it perfectly aligned with how, within Hillsong, Brian Houston centralised power and constructed a system that put him beyond accountability— excepting that of God.

Morrison's leadership style mirrored the absolute authority enjoyed by a senior pastor. He made it clear that he would not be bound by the advice of bureaucrats, a position which undermined transparency and accountability. It white-anted the effective processes established over decades for providing expert, unbiased advice to government.

Morrison was addicted to secrecy. It started with his time as immigration minister, when his refusal to discuss 'on-water matters' was an effective means of avoiding legitimate questions about his own and his department's decisions and actions. And this hostility to the idea that citizens have a right to know what their government is doing persisted throughout his time as prime minister. He told lies and shifted his position, doing so with no sense of shame so long as it maintained his power.

The former PM detests independent processes, and was forever acting to undermine the ability of agencies with oversight responsibilities to perform their authorised duties. The list of examples is long, from his stacking of independent government authorities with political friends, to his disdain for the Australian National Audit Office, which has the job of interrogating how the government spends public money. Morrison resisted the establishment of an independent federal integrity commission.

Morrison, in other words, was party to the destruction of the very processes that define a healthy democratic government. What remained was the appearance of democracy via elections every three years—something he believed he was very good at.

The argument that Morrison was acting like any Liberal politician only goes so far. In reality, he operated as an extremist—so much so that many in his own party, at time of writing, want him out of the parliament.

It was only after Morrison was booted out of office that the truth came to light of the extent of his disdain for the processes of secular democracy. As we saw earlier in this book, Morrison had assumed the powers of five ministerial positions in a period of just over a year. No one, including Morrison himself, has been able to offer a coherent or plausible explanation for this. His excuse was that he wanted to be in a position to immediately assume control, should a minister be incapacitated by Covid-19, but this was not necessary constitutionally.

Morrison chose not to present himself for a formal interview at an inquiry conducted by former High Court justice Virginia Bell. Instead, he made his case through social media statements, a media conference and a media interview with an interviewer of his choosing. The Bell Inquiry ultimately found that Morrison's explanations didn't add up. The one time he'd used the ministerial powers he had assumed, it was to boost the Coalition's electoral chances by cancelling an unpopular resources development—nothing to do with Covid.

The self-appointments were bizarre and unprecedented. Commentators called his behaviour desperate and delusional. Morrison saw himself as a Moses figure, and it is as credible an explanation as any that it was this view that dictated his actions. His own colleagues described him as being messianic.

An open question is whether or not he acted out of the particular Pentecostal belief that the end times were upon us and that it was time for the godly to assume the levers of government, in preparation for the second coming. There is no doubt that Morrison saw in Covid the potential for catastrophic consequences. He spoke of this more than once, including at a tumultuous press conference where he attempted to justify his ministry grab by referring to 'the prospect of serious loss of life, of disruption to civil society, of the collapse of our economy'.

To a Christian with an end-of-days belief, it must surely have looked like God's time had arrived. To a Pentecostal prime minister, who had been told by his religious mentor that he was a Moses figure and who believed that God had a plan for him to lead, there is some logic to interpreting the coming of the fires, then the plague and then the floods as a sign that he should take control of the agencies of government.

Morrison's fellow Pentecostal believer Stuart Robert sat alongside him in cabinet. Robert was the Minister for Employment, Workforce, Skills, Small and Family Business, and had been appointed Acting Minister for Education in December 2021 following the resignation of Alan Tudge. With five major ministries in his back pocket, Morrison had devised a situation where two Pentecostal men controlled a majority of government agencies—even if one of them might not have known that.

Bell found that Morrison's deeds had corroded public trust in the democratic system—an extraordinary judgement on the man who was at the very pinnacle of government and, in theory, the custodian of Australia's democratic system.

No one dared to publicly venture that Australia's prime minister was so religiously cooked that it made sense to him to prepare for the end times.

The Media Misses the Story

Two remarkable artworks hung in Scott Morrison's prime ministerial office. One was a magnificent framed photograph of a soaring eagle. The other was a painting of a river red gum tree on the bank of the Darling River. Both were quintessentially Australian works. Any visitor to Canberra might have thought that here was a prime minister with an eye for Australian art and a keen interest in the natural world.

In reality, it's more complicated than that. To the owner of these artworks, each was a modern-day religious symbol.

The photograph of the soaring eagle, as described earlier, came from the gallery of photographer Ken Duncan. Duncan is a Christian who has his own backstory of miracles and a life changed by God. When Morrison saw the photograph during the 2019 election campaign, he famously saw it as a message from God to keep on going. Morrison was rewarded with the miracle election win.

Less attention has been given to the painting of the river red gum on the Darling River by artist Jenny Greentree. Scott Morrison saw it during a visit to Greentree's gallery in Bourke in 2018, when he was the federal treasurer, and he bought it on the spot. Jenny Greentree is a Christian who arrived in Bourke working with a conservative Christian organisation called Cornerstone, which seeks to 'impact the world'. Morrison recalled what the painting meant to him during his sermon on the topic of anxiety at Margaret Court's Victory Life Centre.

'I was there doing some things on the drought,' he said. '[The gallery] was run by this wonderful Christian woman and her husband, who had beautiful artworks. And I saw this wonderful picture that she painted from the district of this beautiful old gum tree on the side of a flowing river. And it reminded me of this verse: "Blessed is the one who trusts in the Lord, and whose trust is in the Lord. For thy will be like a tree planted by the water that extends its roots by a stream and does not fear when the heat comes. But its leaves will be green and it will not be anxious in a year of drought nor cease to yield fruit."'

How the Australian prime minister's office became a shrine to Christian symbolism is quite a story. It shows the two worlds that Morrison has inhabited simultaneously. The one seen by the public at large is that of a suburban, cap-wearing footy fan and daggy dad; the other is an intense, symbol-laden world of deep spiritual conviction that he shares with a small minority of Australians.

It begs the question: how could the media have missed the story, which was there in plain sight all along? Where was the mighty Canberra press corps as Morrison spoke of miracles and wonders and performed somersaults to look after his mate Brian Houston?

———

With the Hillsong prime minister having dispensed with secular accountability, it was left to Australia's media organisations— the 'fourth estate'—to provide accountability. Yet they failed comprehensively to come to terms with what the rise of Scott Morrison meant.

Maybe Morrison just got lucky. He came to power at a time of a weakening in traditional media in Australia. It's hard to imagine that Morrison would have survived a more rigorous era of political journalism. Any prime minister speaking of miracles and soaring eagles would likely have been torn to shreds by seasoned reporters like Alan Ramsey or Richard Carleton.

Even so, shouldn't it ring journalists' alarm bells that a prime minister claims victory because of a miracle—God's intervention—all the while forgetting the dirty tricks, the lies and the scare tactics that actually tipped the balance?

Who knows if Scott Morrison took the advice of the American televangelist and arch-conservative politician Pat Robertson, but it certainly looks like he did. In a memo titled 'How to participate in a political party', Robertson exhorted his followers to 'Rule the world for God', 'Give the impression that you are there to work for the party, not push an ideology', 'Hide your strength' and 'Don't flaunt your Christianity'.

'Christians need to take leadership positions,' he wrote. 'Party officers control political parties and so it is very important that mature Christians have a majority of leadership whenever possible, God willing.'

There is ample evidence that Morrison publicly curated his image so as to present a far milder version of his Christianity than was the case. For his entire pre–prime ministerial career, he was happy to foster the perception that he was an unexceptional Christian, the follower of a mainstream religion, just like anyone else—a sensible man who knew very well not to mix his religion and politics. In so doing, he obscured those years of his life spent in a fringe movement which has an end-times theology.

In 2015, when Morrison was rising through the ranks of the governing Liberal Party, he told the ABC's Annabel Crabb that he had grown up in the Uniting Church and later gone to a local Pentecostal church, which might be similar to Hillsong but ran under its own rules. It was merely a 'local community church' in the same denomination as Hillsong. 'These churches are incredibly mainstream,' he asserted.

Morrison largely maintained this public image of himself while prime minister. Once he had been voted out of office, though, another version emerged. He spoke in more detail about his life in the Christian Brethren, a vastly different proposition from the Uniting Church. The Christian Brethren—even the open version—is regarded as fringe by most Christians.

Morrison, it turned out, had gone there as a teenager. When he was in his late teens, his brother, Alan, baptised him at the Christian Brethren Assembly at Waverley Gospel Chapel, which is where Scott met his wife, Jenny. After attending university and undertaking his major research project on the growth of Sydney's Christian Brethren churches, he was still attending the Christian Brethren church a decade later, when he worked in New Zealand. He and Jenny went to church at the Christchurch Brethren Assembly, which, he said, was 'a lot more charismatic' in style.

Luckily for Scott Morrison, the cream of Australia's political commentariat and journalists looked at the Christian-Lite package and bought the idea that he was just an overweight, balding, middle-aged bloke from the suburbs, married with two children. He didn't come off as too educated, and liked to wear baseball caps and kick a ball around. Not only did they buy it, they even adopted Morrison's self-appointed nickname, 'ScoMo', and magnified the hokey everyman image he was trying to project.

Morrison proceeded with an acute awareness that the broader Australian public didn't want religion and politics to mix. He always insisted, with a jaw-jutting determination, that his religion did not influence his politics. 'The Bible is not a policy handbook, and I get very worried when people try to treat it like one,' he said—though at the same time he was presenting the opposite message to his Pentecostal fellow travellers.

Perhaps the Canberra press gallery considered that Scott Morrison was religious in the same way that former prime ministers Tony Abbott, Kevin Rudd and John Howard were religious. Each of them represented a different strand of Christianity, all of them traditional: Abbott was a Catholic, Rudd an Anglican turned Catholic, and Howard an Anglican. Yet they were cut from a very different religious cloth.

Morrison benefited from having the dominant media organisation, News Corporation, in his corner and utterly committed to supporting him, come what may. He also benefited from a cautious ABC, which had been cowed by a decade or more of constant attacks by the Coalition parties. Imagine the national broadcaster daring to wade into Morrison's private religious world!

It is accepted among journalists that a politician's religion is a private matter, and off-limits to the public. However, Morrison opened the door to having his beliefs examined when he made his religion a public matter. During the 2019 election campaign, he made a photo-op visit to his local Pentecostal church, where he was pictured with hands held aloft, receiving the Holy Spirit.

In truth, Morrison left a very long trail of breadcrumbs, which showed how important his beliefs were to him and how they influenced his political decision-making. Those venerable insiders of the Canberra press corps, though, remained stoically incurious about what it all meant.

Alarmingly, those paid to know how power works in Canberra were as shocked as anyone when the disclosures tumbled out— after Morrison had lost office—about his secret grab of five ministries under the cover of Covid-19. Morrison had spent fifteen years in public life, yet it was as though no one in the Canberra gallery knew him at all.

It is hard to unravel Scott Morrison if you don't understand the Pentecostal world he comes from. And it is outright impossible if you can't imagine the profound nature of religious belief on the part of Pentecostal Christians—especially of the kind peddled by the charismatic and enormously successful Brian Houston.

10
AMEN

Judgment Day

Almost 25 years after Brian Houston learnt of his father's crimes against a young Brett Sengstock, a Sydney court delivered its judgment on whether or not Australia's highest-profile Pentecostal leader was guilty of the crime of concealment, given he did not report what he knew to police.

Concealment is classed as a serious indictable offence under Section 316 of the *Crimes Act*, New South Wales. The offence was said to have occurred between 15 September 1999 and 9 November 2004, when Frank Houston died.

After a marathon hearing which raked over decades-old recollections from a procession of Pentecostal figures, Sydney magistrate Gareth Christofi ruled that the crown had failed to prove its case beyond a reasonable doubt.

It took the magistrate one and a half hours to deliver his reasoning to a central Sydney court bursting at the seams with lawyers and journalists, as well Brett Sengstock's supporters, a smattering of Pentecostal pastors and members of the public curious to learn the fate of the celebrity preacher who had dominated the national stage for years.

Magistrate Christofi moved methodically through the pillars of the crown case finding that, one by one, the prosecution had failed to meet the high standard of proof required to establish Houston's guilt and send him to prison for potentially three to five years.

Perhaps principal among these was that Brett Sengstock himself had not wanted the police to be involved back in 1999. This was a primary plank in the 'reasonable excuse' case advanced by Houston, who had said all along that he was respecting the victim's wishes.

The magistrate also accepted Houston's argument that Sengstock could have gone to the police himself if he wished given he was an adult in his late thirties in 1999 when information on the historic sex abuse emerged.

The magistrate found that the $10,000 paid to Sengstock in a deal done by Frank Houston and Nabi Saleh at a McDonald's outlet was not hush money. 'I cannot be satisfied (that) the payment of this money was an attempt to silence Mr Sengstock as opposed to some kind of informal form of financial compensation,' he ruled.

Magistrate Christofi also found decisively against the crown argument that Brian Houston had attempted to hide information on the crime.

'Indeed the evidence was that he had told many people at various levels of the Assemblies of God and within his own church of exactly what his father had done.

'Whilst the accused may have been euphemistic at times, when speaking to large gatherings of thousands of people, it would have been perfectly obvious to anyone, what he was talking about. Anyone who was left wondering needed only to ask around to obtain the details about what the accused was referring to.

'Secondly, the obvious conclusion to be drawn from the fact that the accused was speaking of the issue publicly to his congregation, speaking to those watching the television broadcasts of these sermons around the world, and speaking to journalists, is that he wanted people to know about it.

'That is the very opposite of a cover up,' the magistrate ruled.

The magistrate found this to be the case even though, as disclosed earlier in this book, some of Brian Houston's public statements appear to have left the impression that his father's criminal act had occurred in New Zealand rather than Sydney, therefore placing it outside the reach of the New South Wales police.

With that, Brian Houston was in the clear. It had been ten years since the McClellan Inquiry had referred the Sengstock issue for investigation by New South Wales police and two years since he had been charged with the crime of concealment in 2021, forcing him to stand aside from his role as global senior pastor at Hillsong Church.

The resounding court victory brought a form of redemption for Houston and a weight off his shoulders, but it came way too late to mend his relationship with Hillsong Church.

By the time of the court verdict, Hillsong, seemingly from top to bottom, was well and truly done with Brian Houston.

They had made their judgement on other grounds. For some the revelation of Houston's improper dealings with two women were serious moral transgressions and enough to cut him loose. For others it was Houston's drinking. In the US Houston had been charged and convicted of drunk driving as his trial played out in Sydney. Beyond that were the whistleblower revelations of the high life which the Houstons enjoyed, using the vast sums of money given sacrificially by ordinary Hillsong parishioners as well as the Kingdom Builders.

Hillsong's leadership had made its judgement on Houston and it had little to do with allegations that Houston had covered up for his father's crimes.

In an odd twist, the Sengstock case and Houston's acquittal proved that the findings of the secular courts were indeed meaningless for Hillsong's Christian followers. They considered that they were guided by a higher moral standard than is to be found in the secular courts. It is by that standard which Houston had failed.

———

In the aftermath of his acquittal Brian Houston remained, to his despair, an outsider to the organisation he had built.

On the Sunday following the court decision, Houston publicly thanked those in the wider Pentecostal movement who had acknowledged the not guilty verdict in their church services, during the so-called praise reports.

'Thank you to all those pastors around Australia who told me yesterday there was a public praise report for my vindication,'

Houston tweeted. 'But' he lamented, 'in the church we care about the most it didn't rate a mention. It hurts.'

The Houston verdict had been ignored by Hillsong whose global pastor, Phil Dooley, used the church's main Sunday service to sermonise on the failings of leaders who forget that they are followers of the Lord Jesus Christ. Houston was not mentioned by name. There was no need to as Dooley told the story of the errant shepherd who ended up losing his flock.

In response to media inquiries the church issued a short statement which gave no quarter to Houston while offering an unusual degree of empathy for the victims of Frank Houston.

'Hillsong Church acknowledges the decision of the court. Our prayer is that those impacted deeply and irrevocably by the actions of Frank Houston will find peace and healing, and that our former senior pastor Brian Houston and his family can look to the future and continue to fulfil God's purpose for their lives.'

As the great Brian Houston discovered, the vindication he was looking for was an illusion. There was in the end very little to celebrate from the court verdict.

For Brett Sengstock it was another blow. Putting the best face on the not guilty verdict, Sengstock told the media that he had received 'some recognition for a seven-year-old child who was brutally abused at the hands of a self-confessed child rapist and coward, Frank Houston'.

Flanked by supporters Sengstock said that regardless of the result he had been handed a life sentence.

'Frank Houston was no pioneer for Christianity, his legacy remains a faded memory of a paedophile,' Sengstock said.

There was no hero's reception for Houston. He conducted an interview with conservative commentator Andrew Bolt which started from the premise that Houston had been persecuted for being a Christian.

'I genuinely believe that if I wasn't Brian Houston from Hillsong Church, this trial would never have happened. There were many people who were aware of the accusations about my father before I was.

'I think that there is a hostility that comes towards especially prominent pastors, people that are doing something a little different than the norm. And it's a tragic blight, I think, on sections of the Australian media, and sections of the Australian population,' he said.

The interview was also the first time Houston had put forward any public explanation for how he ended up in the hotel room of a female Hillsong supporter for 40 minutes during Hillsong's 2019 conference.

'I knocked on the wrong door,' Houston offered. 'In fact, I knocked on the door next to our [hotel] door. And I thought that person was in our room in the state of confusion that I was in,' he said.

The woman in question complained to Hillsong's senior management about Houston's behaviour and subsequently left the church. Brian Houston repaid her conference fee and returned a donation she had made. She has never spoken publicly about the event.

Of the incident which occurred in 2013 involving texts with a young female employee, Houston told Andrew Bolt he had sent a single text while under the influence of sleeping tablets. The text had referred to hugging and kissing the employee.

'It was a stupid text . . . I was not conscious of—in a state of subconsciousness. And when I woke up in the morning, [I] realised what I'd done. It wasn't something that was done premeditated or anything like that. And I apologised immediately.'

The employee left Hillsong over the incident and was paid a couple of months salary on her way.

Houston conceded he wasn't sure what he and his wife, Bobbie, would do next.

'But I do know I'm too young to retire. And so I hope to make a solid contribution. I love the Lord Jesus Christ. I love serving him. I love people. I love the congregation at Hillsong. We still miss them desperately, and [are] so full of expectation that we're forging something for the future.

'I love Australia. We both love Australia. But Australia, in many ways hasn't loved us. And that makes me very sad. But it's a truth. And so we're in a state of flux. I think we will be spending more time overseas where potentially there's a lot more opportunity for us,' he concluded.

It was a hell of a way to mark the fortieth anniversary of Hillsong's operations, a milestone which happened to fall in the very week Houston was acquitted and left fully abandoned by his church.

Was It All Just a Bad Dream?

Amid the collapsing rubble of Hillsong lie a hundred cautionary tales involving the believers who saw their dreams turn to ash.

Just one is the experience of a pastor's wife, Faye, who devoted the best years of her life to saving souls for Jesus. Her story underlines the cult-like power of the closed church community, locked in an us-versus-them struggle with the outside world.

Faye was educated at a Christian school in Queensland. She married her youth leader. He was 21 and she was seventeen. The two had been in a secret relationship, and when the church found out about it, they were shamed in front of the local congregation. If they wanted to follow their natural urges, as it were, they would have to do so in the God-sanctified union of marriage.

Faye, the faithful Pentecostal church attender, would come to know the business of saving souls from all sides. One day her husband received a message from God that the family—they now had three children—should move from Brisbane to 'plant' a church in the Bible belt of Dallas, Texas. The new church was to be affiliated with a large Pentecostal church, Wave Church, which was part of the Hillsong family of churches internationally. Wave was led by an Australian, Pastor Steve Kelly, a one-time close colleague of Brian Houston's who had been on Hillsong's staff for a decade. Carl Lentz—later the New York City celebrity pastor—made the odd visit out to Faye's church in Texas.

Faye spent some of the best years of her life inside the Pentecostal mindset. She entered the church in 1989 and left in 2008 after suffering burnout in Texas, where the pressure was on to build church attendances, with little real support. Faye had been dux of her school, but going on to university was not on the radar for the young pastor's wife. There was urgent work to be done for Jesus. 'You don't hold high regard for worldly things like university,' she recalls. 'It's all about saving souls. So even though I was accepted into uni, I was almost discouraged to do that because it was more about building the church and supporting my husband, as a pastor. And the church is very much about both of you pastoring.'

The concept of salvation is a cornerstone belief. It also separates a believer from the rest. 'The thing that I find interesting is, when you're in the church—this is probably the Pentecostal culture in particular—you have this real sense that you're saved,' Faye says. 'And when I say saved, you're going to heaven when you pass away. You have a relationship with God, you've invited him into your heart.'

Being immersed in a Pentecostal community meant Faye lived a life separated from the mainstream of society. 'You are surrounded by Christians,' she explains. 'And that's all you talk about. You know, you talk about the power of God, you talk about the Bible, and you talk about all of these things. And so, when you interact with non-Christians, which isn't too often, you have this real sense, this quiet confidence, of self-righteousness—that you've got it right and that you are superior to those you're talking to because you're going to heaven, and they're not yet going to go to heaven.

'And so you need to kind of get that message across, but you try and come across in a very humble way. But it's surface-level humility, because, deep down, it's like, "I've got it right and you don't have it right." It sounds like a smugness, I guess, and you can see that when you talk to a Christian even now.

'I know there's a lot of really genuine people in the church. And I also know that the church is a fantastic place for lonely people to go, or for people with low self-esteem. Because every week they're under these teachings that they're special for God. And God's going to do great things. And God loves them with all their flaws. And so it's such a fantastic, rewarding part of the church. And I really wish that the ugly part wasn't there.'

It is unusual for a church insider to speak publicly about their experience, let alone to be critical. Like others, Faye has friends and family she doesn't want to hurt. There is also a powerful prohibition about speaking to a non-believer about such questions, as though it is a betrayal of the godly community.

Being the wife of a pastor means having a joint responsibility for the finances of the church. The getting of money—or 'the Sunday stick-up', as it is derisively known—is fundamental to that. It has been honed to perfection in the Hillsong setting.

This, from Faye, an insider, is how it works. 'Whoever was rostered on to do the offering would really prepare. They'd pray and come with this really dynamic, powerful message "from God" around taking the offering. So it wasn't just slipped into the service. It is a really passionate message, and it gets people's emotions really high about giving. That's every week.

'And then they'd also have the building fund. So they'd encourage you to do pledges.

'If there was a visiting pastor, they always take up a love offering at the end, where they pass the basket around and the pastor of the church would say we should bless this man of God, who's given up his time to be with us. With a thousand people in the congregation, it could add up to a lot of money. And obviously it wasn't taxed or anything.'

More than ten years after she left, Faye still questions the truth of some of the Pentecostal practices she lived by. 'You'd have to pray and pray in tongues, and I'd speak in tongues about being baptised in the Holy Spirit. You pray for people, and they'd kind of fall down under the power of God. That's what I thought at the time. And now I don't even know how to make sense of that, to be completely honest. Now I look back, I'm like, maybe I was just making it up. It was just words that you hear other people say.'

Faye has come to hold doubts about falling backwards as the pastor places their hand on the head of a worshipper—the practice known as 'being slain in the Holy Spirit'.

'Now, looking back, I'm wondering: was that hysteria? I mean, I have fallen backwards and I think I felt something, but I'm not sure. But maybe it is the power of suggestion that makes you feel that. I still don't know.'

Faye and her husband parted ways after a bruising two years in Dallas. It also meant the end of her time in the church. But leaving was a hard and scarring experience. 'That's your whole support system,' she explains. 'So I'd lost money because we put all our money into the church. And then you lost your faith. And you lost your friends and your support network. Your identity. And, you know, your whole world comes crashing down.

'So actually leaving the church is a really big thing. Because it's you leaving everything that you've known to be real, and you're leaving your way of life.

'And then, of course, when you have left, people look at you as a backslidden Christian. You go out, and if people know that you've been in the church there, and they're Christians, you can see them trying to make an effort to get you back into the church by giving you a Bible or being really pitiful. They think you are defective, that you've somehow got it wrong.'

After twenty years on the inside and coping with the strains of a loss of identity, Faye still can't quite fathom what happened.

A smart, high-achieving young woman found herself as the collateral damage of a powered-for-Jesus movement which relied ultimately on the slave labour of a pastor's wife.

It was a long way from the image promoted by the church of the happy Hillsong couple working together to build the kingdom.

Apocalypse Now

Plenty of people will take comfort, if not joy, in the demise of the Houstons and the old Hillsong.

Frank and Brian Houston made enemies as they clawed their way to the top of Australian Pentecostalism. The higher the Houstons rose, the more power they wielded. And the more powerful they became, the more they silenced dissent.

Critics learnt that they would be crushed if they got in the way.

One church leader emerged as an opponent of the Houstons and all they stood for. The story of Philip Powell has been missing in the accounts of the rise and fall of Hillsong, but in the great morality play of the last several decades he has been an inspiration to a small dissident movement within Pentecostalism.

Powell was once at the top of the pile, as general secretary of the Assemblies of God in Australia. He resigned in 1992, as the Houston machine cranked up. He believed the church was preaching false doctrines and supporting false prophets and teachers. He, too, had started his career in New Zealand, and he was more than familiar with the Houstons' modus operandi from their early days.

Powell made a stand against the growing greed ethos of Australian Pentecostalism. He flooded other church leaders with warnings of the wrongs being done by the Houstons. He went public in the early 2000s about the celebrity Pentecostal speaking circuit, and the arrangement was finally exposed in the trove of whistleblower documents tabled in Australia's federal parliament in 2023.

Powell also publicly charged that there was a pervasive culture of cover-up of sexual immorality in the Australian and New Zealand Assemblies of God governing bodies. That, too, was in the early 2000s, when the national executive of the Assemblies of God were busy putting the best possible spin on Frank Houston's crimes.

There is evidence that in the years before he went public, Philip Powell attempted to alert others in the Pentecostal move-ment of rumours about Frank Houston's sex crimes in New Zealand. This was in the days before mobile phones and the internet, and he did so by sending reams of faxes to Assemblies of God churches.

On one account, when confronted with these claims, Frank Houston denied Powell's information outright and accused him of being motivated by jealousy. That was in the mid-1980s, as the Houstons were cementing their place in Sydney.

Frank Houston then set out to destroy the reputation of Philip Powell, who set up his own watchdog ministry, called Christian Witness Ministries, essentially to monitor Hillsong.

The demonising of Powell was complete. Others in the Pentecostal movement dismissed him as a malcontent for years after Frank Houston died.

It only became apparent that Powell had been telling the truth in 2014, when the details of Frank Houston's offending were revealed at the royal commission. It was the moment when Brian Houston revealed that he had declined to meet a victim of his father's abuse because Powell—'a well-known mischief-maker', as Houston called him—had been advocating on the victim's behalf.

In the small world of Pentecostalism, that royal commission moment was a blinding revelation for a regional New South Wales pastor called Bob Cotton, who had believed until then that Frank Houston had been guilty of nothing more than patting a young man on the bottom, a one-off indiscretion in the dim, dark past in New Zealand.

Pastor Cotton, like pretty well everyone else in Australian Pentecostalism, had also bought the line that Philip Powell was nothing more than a troublemaker.

'I was programmed to believe that Philip Powell was the enemy,' he says, explaining that 'enemy' was religious code for Satan. Powell was also portrayed by the Houstons and their acolytes at the top of Australian Pentecostalism as 'bitter'—another codeword for the work of Satan.

The programming began as far back as 2000, when the Pentecostal church hierarchy sent a letter to all pastors about Frank Houston's 'moral failing' and its decision to forbid him from pastoring again. Sent on Christmas Eve and marked 'Extremely Confidential', the instruction was for pastors to keep the grim news of the great Frank Houston to themselves. There was no need to announce it to their church 'or further afield', given there was always 'one or two people with their own agendas'—a clear reference again to Philip Powell.

Pastor Cotton remembers the moment that fifteen years of deception about Frank Houston was blown away. 'I felt gutted like a fish,' he says. 'You know, the bottom's fallen out of the bag. The world's come apart.'

Bob Cotton had looked up to Frank Houston as a hero of the church. What's more, Houston and his wife, Hazel, had been honoured guests in Cotton's home. As the pastor heard the details of how Frank Houston had preyed on seven-year-old Brett Sengstock, he was sickened at what might have occurred in his own home. At the time of Frank Houston's visits, the Cottons' son was eight years of age.

'I looked back at what happened and it was clear that Frank Houston was working his way into our life and our family. He groomed us and our son.

'He gave gifts to our son—he always seized the opportunity to pray for Ben, to lay hands on him, to flatter Ben and make out that he thought our son was special and that God was upon our son for greatness and all this sort of business.'

It was, Bob Cotton learnt, all part of the Houston modus operandi. The great pastor even had special Mont Blanc copy pens made up with 'Frank Houston' printed on the side to give to all the kids.

The royal commission's revelations proved that Philip Powell had been correct all along—and that he had been vilified to protect the good name of Frank Houston.

Bob Cotton has a saying that captures what he came to understand as the courage of Philip Powell in standing up to the Houston juggernaut: 'God uses good men, and bad men use God.'

That moment of revelation set Bob Cotton on a path of seeking to expose the Hillsong Church leadership who, he considers, failed utterly to deliver any form of justice to Frank Houston's victims.

He sums it up: 'Unfortunately, they offer grace to the perpetrator while the law is applied to the victim.'

When Philip Powell died in 2015, an anonymous group behind an online organisation called Churchwatch quietly marked his passing as 'one of the few faithful Pentecostal ministers we know, who dared stand against the onslaught of false teaching overwhelming Australian and New Zealand Christianity. May his work be remembered, cherished and used as a strong warning against the rising corruption coming against the body of Christ.'

Once Bob Cotton saw the light on the Houstons, he too found himself on the outer with the power players of the Pentecostal movement.

Over the years that became an ever-expanding club.

———

Brian Houston set out to make a church that didn't look, smell, sound or act like a church. He succeeded, wildly. But, ultimately, so much of it was an illusion.

Hillsong looked modern, hip and happening. You could love the Lord and love money at the same time. You could drive an Audi, have a big white smile and wear a $40,000 wristwatch and still have Jesus' blessing. How good is Hillsong!

The church's entrepreneurial spirit matched what was occurring in the home of evangelical Pentecostalism, the United States. It aligned them perfectly and absolutely with the free-enterprise ethos of the Liberal Party of Australia. As much as any bare-knuckle capitalist enterprise, the Houston brand has relied on aggressive expansion, fuelled by taking over other, distressed churches and relentlessly seeking to grow the pie. It has relied on paying out as little as possible to the thousands of Hillsong followers who 'volunteer' to 'serve'. The business model also relies on the regulatory leniency of governments.

In 2022 Hillsong hit the wall. It collided with the 21st century and, when the curtain was swept back, it revealed an organisation addicted to secrecy, run on cronyism and dead against secular accountability. Hillsong was, in fact, an old-fashioned paternalistic organisation, run by greed, where women had no effective voice.

The numbers tell the story of a collapsing edifice. In the church's heyday, it ran at least three services on Sundays at its Sydney HQ in the Hills District, where thousands at a time could be accommodated. That has since dwindled to one service.

That, in itself, marks a tipping point. The church needs enough numbers to generate the surging crowd energy that defined a Hillsong gathering. Otherwise, you might be left with the same yawning emptiness of any other church.

The new, post-Houston Hillsong is already a far cry from its thumping all-entertainment predecessor. Its global pastor, Phil Dooley, speaks of a 'healthy' church. This means no more VIP areas where those who give the most money get the best access to Brian Houston. It means the end of the pay-to-play style of Christianity which Hillsong led in Australia.

Hillsong without Brian Houston is a more muted affair. Its crop of preachers are no match for Houston's energy and presence. Showtime is not what it used to be.

In its place is a lower-wattage performance, with pastors who tell a wholesome story in smart casual clothes but lack Houston's power to dominate the stage and capture an audience.

The new Hillsong takes expert advice from governance consultants rather than follow the instincts of its one-time ruler. To that extent it has followed a path trodden by other family-owned businesses which have become large national enterprises.

There has been radical change to Hillsong's board of directors bringing it more in line with 21st-century corporate governance. For its entire existence the Hillsong board under Houston was nearly all male with members drawn from Houston's inner circle. By late 2023 the eight-member Hillsong board was made up of four women and four men. One director, Dr Robyn Ober, is a Mamu/Djirribal woman from North Queensland and a member of Hillsong's recently created Racial Equity Committee.

This change at the top put an end to the one-man-rule style of Brian Houston. Suddenly the leadership looks more like the body of the church, with different perspectives having value. If Hillsong is a changed church then much of that is due to the actions of individuals like whistleblower Natalie Moses and her husband, Glen. The two paid a high price for shining a light on the dark corners of the megachurch and its finances. Was it worth it?

Stripped of old friendships and ostracised from a church life he loved, Glen Moses struggles to answer that question. 'Even though we've taken some knocks over this, I know that's done so much good for a lot of people,' he says. 'What we've done has benefited other people in positive ways. There's so many people that feel validated now about the things they were feeling and the experiences they were going through. So that's good. I feel good about the whole thing.'

The field is littered with others who took on the Houston machine, both publicly and privately. Many of these individuals have spoken to me but asked to keep their names out of the public domain, for fear of retribution or simply because they want to get on with their new lives. The internet has allowed disillusioned Hillsong followers to gather in secure online communities, arming each other—and journalists—with information. The empire the Houstons built was an extraordinary Australian success story—a tale of self-made fortune propelled by powerful, pioneering founders who came to enjoy political patronage at the highest levels. Ultimately, it collapsed under the weight of its own moral failings, and its two-tiered system which delivered wealth and special treatment to a relative handful of individuals clustered around the Houstons.

In the end Brian Houston has had a taste of his own medicine. Hillsong has turned on its maker, leaving him and Bobbie Houston with the deeply demoralising feeling that comes with being shunned by the church they loved.

The ugly divorce from the church will likely not leave the Houstons out of pocket. There have been reports of a seven-figure settlement for Bobbie Houston and an undisclosed package for Brian. There is also the prospect of royalties continuing to flow to the Houstons from Hillsong music.

The cutting of ties, though, has embittered Brian Houston, who has railed against the pygmies who have brought him down. It was all summed up in one angry jab by Houston at those who expelled him and his wife, Bobbie, made in a late 2022 gathering with supporters: 'Ultimately God called Bobbie and I to Sydney . . . We were never called by a board—we were called by God. So God will be the one who tells us where we go from here.'

Without the backing of the glorious Hillsong enterprise, the founding pastor has had to make do with social media platforms to vent his anger and disappointment.

The youthful pastor of 40 years ago is well gone. As much as he has sought to resist it, the legendary Brian Houston is now set to join the other prosperity evangelists of his era, fading to black somewhere in the United States, though with the comfort of a well-paid gig or two to keep him in the style to which he has become accustomed.

ACKNOWLEDGEMENTS

In the writing of this book I have benefited enormously from inside information passed to me by several former Hillsong followers. It was immediately clear to me that their motives were the best they could be: to make Hillsong a properly functioning Christian institution, free of hypocrisy and power. These people were working to save the church from itself, yet they would not be thanked for that. Rather they would be marginalised and shunned by their community.

They have shown enormous courage. I would like to thank them for providing their insights and for the advance warning of some key events.

As an outsider to the world of Pentecostal Christianity I found the work of Pentecostal historian Barry Chant to be invaluable, in particular the historic references which he gathered for his PhD thesis (see sources).

I have had long conversations with former and current Christians who have explained the meanings behind some oft-recurring phrases in Pentecostal Christianity. In particular I want to acknowledge Cara Phillips, who is thoroughly versed in that special code known as Christianese. Cara knows the Pentecostal world inside out, having been raised a Christian and ultimately becoming the key whistleblower on decades of serious religious-based abuse taking place inside Perth's Esther Foundation. Cara offered invaluable comments on an early book draft. Similarly Alec Spencer, a lawyer and former Assemblies of God insider, offered fabulous insights into the operation of Basic Religious Charities, the subject of his ground-breaking PhD studies.

I am indebted to Private Media, the owner of the online publication *Crikey*, for giving me the backing to pursue the multi-layered story of Brian Houston and Hillsong as well as to probe the relationship between the pastor and former prime minister, Scott Morrison. Other media by and large shied away from these areas, in particular the idea that a prime minister's decisions might be influenced or dictated by religious belief.

As a glance at the sources for this book will confirm, *Crikey* published large amounts of material which have informed this book.

I am grateful to *Crikey*'s then editor-in-chief, Peter Fray, who provided brilliant leadership for my coverage of this and other important national stories. Peter also offered incisive comments on early drafts of the book. I also want to acknowledge the driving role, too, of Eric Beecher who established the conditions to pursue the important work of investigative journalism at *Crikey*.

I want to acknowledge Allen & Unwin's consultant publisher Richard Walsh for grasping the significance of the rise and fall of Hillsong and its overlap with the rising influence of the religious right in Australian public life. Richard served up a sparkling first edit of the manuscript, providing the framework for the story to unfold.

Finally, I am indebted to the great journalism and story-telling mind of Bronwen Reid. Bronwen provided comments on each chapter as they rolled off the laptop and managed to put her finger on exactly what was missing. Bronwen is an accomplished investigative journalist having worked at the top level in New Zealand and Australia. She is also my wife.

SOURCES

Video

Brian Houston interviewed, Hope 103.2, 9 July 2015: www.youtube.
com/watch?v=Re6GlQzHbFs&list=RDLVRe6GlQzHbFs&
start_radio=1

Brian Houston, 2017 Hillsong Conference: www.youtube.com/
watch?v=PIqq-Tu0AN8

Brian Houston, Scott Morrison, 2019 Hillsong Conference:
www.youtube.com/watch?v=pUg88oftyi8&t=700s

'An evening with Brian and Bobbie Houston', 9 November 2022:
www.facebook.com/watch/live/?ref=watch_permalink&v=
476946374204758

'Hillsong founder talks about "devastating" claims against his
father' (2002), *ABC News*, 21 December 2022: www.abc.net.au/
news/2022-12-21/hillsong-founder-on-how-he-felt-after-the/
101797752

Andrew Bolt interviews Brian Houston, *The Bolt Report*, Sky News
Australia, 18 August 2023: www.youtube.com/watch?v=Nfif
AqcEyOY

Audio Interviews

Bruce Baird on Scott Morrison, Hope 103.2, 27 August 2018:
hope1032.com.au/stories/life/news/2018/new-pm-scott-morrison-
a-genuine-christian-who-wont-backstab-but-a-harsh-stance-on-
refugees/

Carey Nieuwhof interviews Brian Houston, Connexus Church,
7 October 2018: connexuschurch.libsyn.com/bonus-episode-carey-
nieuwhof-interviews-hillsong-lead-pastor-brian-houston-on-burnout

Print/Text

Greg Bearup, 'Praise the Lord and pass the chequebook', Good
Weekend, *Sydney Morning Herald*, 25 January 2003: www.smh.
com.au/national/praise-the-lord-and-pass-the-chequebook-
20050218-gdkrdq.html

'The lord's profits', *Sydney Morning Herald*, 30 January 2003: www.
smh.com.au/national/the-lords-profits-20030130-gdg6nb.html

Carolyn Tuft and Bill Smith, 'From Fenton to fortune in the name of
God', *St. Louis Post-Dispatch*, 15 November 2003: web.archive.
org/web/20071011071211/http://www.stltoday.com/stltoday/
news/special/joycemeyer.nsf/story/C5099399D2FCC5F
A86256DDF00661C5F?OpenDocument

'In God they trust', *Sydney Morning Herald*, 12 April 2004: www.
smh.com.au/national/in-god-they-trust-20040412-gdipuk.html

'Hillsong farewells a lost sheep pioneer', *Sydney Morning Herald*,
13 November 2004: www.smh.com.au/national/hillsong-
farewells-a-lost-sheep-pioneer-20041113-gdk3uq.html

Ruth Pollard, 'They prayed to cast Satan from my body', *The Age*,
17 March 2008: www.theage.com.au/national/they-prayed-to-
cast-satan-from-my-body-20080317-ge6uur.html

Ruth Pollard, 'Mercy Ministries home to close', *Sydney Morning
Herald*, 28 October 2009: www.smh.com.au/national/mercy-
ministries-home-to-close-20091027-hj2k.html

Ruth Pollard 'Mercy Ministries admits claims were false', *Sydney
Morning Herald*, 17 December 2009: www.smh.com.au/national/
mercy-ministries-admits-claims-were-false-20091216-kxl4.html

Adam Shand, 'Taxpayers support lavish Hillsong lifestyle', *Sunday Telegraph*, 25 July 2010: www.dailytelegraph.com.au/taxpayers-support-lavish-hillsong-lifestyle/news-story/25af3a860c70628c87 4389e90d33917b

Juliet Rieden, 'We're not a cult', *Australian Women's Weekly*, March 2016

Janet Fife-Yeoman, 'Frank Houston tried to buy forgiveness from victim in deal drawn up on McDonald's napkin', *Daily Telegraph*, 10 October 2014: www.dailytelegraph.com.au/news/nsw/frank-houston-tried-to-buy-forgiveness-from-victim-in-deal-drawn-up-on-mcdonalds-napkin/news-story/24f42dcdf0ff4a12ea059e0ca7 aed437

Rachel Browne, 'Paedophile pastor could have many more victims, royal commission hears', *Sydney Morning Herald*, 10 October 2014: www.smh.com.au/national/paedophile-pastor-could-have-many-more-victims-royal-commission-hears-20141010-114bu3.html

Rachel Browne, 'Royal Commission sex abuse inquiry censures Hillsong head Brian Houston, *Sydney Morning Herald*, 23 November 2015: www.smh.com.au/national/nsw/royal-commission-sex-abuse-inquiry-censures-hillsong-head-brian-houston-20151123-gl5esn.html

Tess Delbridge, '"God became toxic to me," says Mercy Ministries graduate', *Eternity News*, 1 September 2016: www.eternitynews.com.au/in-depth/god-became-toxic-to-me-says-mercy-ministries-graduate/

Leonardo Blair, ' Hillsong Church Becomes Own Denomination, Splits From Australia's Largest Pentecostal Group', *Christian Post*, 19 September 2018: www.christianpost.com/news/hillsong-church-becomes-own-denomination-splits-from-australias-largest-pentecostal-group.html

David Furse-Roberts, 'Slavery no more: Wilberforce and the settlement of Australia', *The Spectator*, 26 January 2018: www.spectator.com.au/2018/01/slavery-no-more-wilberforce-and-the-settlement-of-australia/

Gary Adshead, 'WA Libs' evangelicals likened to "a cancer" by
Federal MP who says they are close to a complete "takeover"',
Perth Now, 13 January 2019: www.perthnow.com.au/news/
religion-and-belief/wa-libs-evangelicals-likened-to-a-cancer-
by-federal-mp-who-says-they-are-close-to-a-complete-takeover-
ng-b881070135z

Lauren Effron, Andrew Paparella and Jeca Taudte, 'The scandals
that brought down the Bakkers, once among US's most famous
televangelists', *ABC News* (USA), 20 December 2019: abcnews.
go.com/US/scandals-brought-bakkers-uss-famous-televangelists/
story?id=60389342

John Sandeman, 'Hillsong is red meat for media: what *60 Minutes*
is serving up this week', *Eternity News*, 18 September 2021:
www.eternitynews.com.au/australia/hillsong-is-red-meat-for-media-
what-60-minutes-is-serving-up-this-week/

David Fisher, 'My Childhood was taken away—the trail of sex abuse
left by top church leaders', *New Zealand Herald*, July 2020:
www.nzherald.co.nz/nz/big-read-trail-of-sex-abuse-left-by-top-
church-leaders-my-childhood-was-taken-away/IHZCVZXV
NKJM27Q37BVTHSQ62I/

David Fisher, 'Assemblies of God leaders alleged to have abused
children', *New Zealand Herald*, 11 July 2020: www.nzherald.
co.nz/nz/assemblies-of-god-leaders-alleged-to-have-abused-
children/HOHUTJGPT5BAHGHJPYUOGFXEVY/

Angeline Jane Bernabe and Kieran McGirl, 'Woman who alleges
affair with former Hillsong Church pastor Carl Lentz speaks
out', *ABC News* (USA), 21 November 2020: abcnews.go.com/
GMA/News/woman-alleges-affair-hillsong-church-pastor-carl-
lentz/story?id=74305467

Donna Lu, 'Hillsong church apologises after investigations find
Brian Houston engaged in "inappropriate" behaviour', *The
Guardian*, 19 March 2022: www.theguardian.com/world/2022/
mar/19/hillsong-church-apologises-after-investigations-find-
brian-houston-engaged-in-inappropriate-behaviour

SOURCES

'Ex-Hillsong leader says . . .', *NewsNation*, 22 April 2022

'"Shame No More" – Brian Houston's sermon after the 2014 Royal Commission Into Child Sexual abuse.', *ChurchWatch*, 6 July 2022: churchwatchcentral.com/2022/07/06/shame-no-more-brian-houstons-sermon-after-the-2014-royal-commission-into-child-sexual-abuse/

Josh Zimmerman and Katina Curtis, 'Goodenough rails against branch stacking in hypocritical email', *West Australian*, 14 October 2022: thewest.com.au/politics/state-politics/prominent-clan-member-and-moore-mp-ian-goodenough-rails-against-branch-stacking-in-hypocritical-email--c-8500623

Stephen Drill, '"Beaten to death": Hillsong lawyer's sexist joke', *Daily Telegraph*, 19 October 2022: www.dailytelegraph.com.au/news/national/beaten-to-death-hillsong-lawyers-sexist-joke/news-story/880c4baf0461019912f983f96d0c1e89

Kurt Mahlberg, 'How William Wilberforce smuggled Revival to Australia', 2 December 2022: kurtmahlburg.blog/2022/12/02/how-william-wilberforce-smuggled-revival-to-australia/

AAP, 'Hillsong manager says church didn't report abuse by Frank Houston as it was not a "current matter", court told', *The Guardian*, 8 December 2022: www.theguardian.com/world/2022/dec/08/hillsong-manager-says-church-didnt-report-abuse-by-frank-houston-as-it-was-not-a-current-matter-court-told

Jack Gramenz, 'Houston "shocked" by abuse report, twice', *Canberra Times*, 8 December 2022: www.canberratimes.com.au/story/8011617/houston-shocked-by-abuse-report-twice/

Heath Parkes-Hupton, 'Brian Houston denies downplaying father's abuse in Hillsong sermon', *ABC News*, 21 December 2022: www.abc.net.au/news/2022-12-21/brian-houston-denies-downplaying-fathers-child-abuse/101797088

Jamie McKinnell and Heath Parkes-Hupton, 'Hillsong founder Brian Houston found not guilty of concealing his father's sexual

289

abuse of a child', *ABC News*, 17 August 2023: www.abc.net.au/news/2023-08-17/hillsong-founder-brian-houston-not-guilty/102740394

Ryan Foley, 'Carl Lentz thanks his wife, Laura, for staying with him, enduring "consequences of my decisions"', *Christian Post*, 20 October 2023: www.christianpost.com/news/carl-lentz-thanks-his-wife-for-not-leaving-him-amid-infidelity.html

Crikey stories by David Hardaker

'Scott Morrison and the Seven Mountains mandate: how the PM is changing Australia in God's name', 27 April 2021: www.crikey.com.au/2021/04/27/scott-morrison-and-the-seven-mountains-mandate-how-the-pm-is-changing-australia-in-gods-name/

'Decoding ScoMo: the hidden story and messages in his Pentecostal mashup', 28 April 2021: www.crikey.com.au/2021/04/28/decoding-scomo-pentecostal-mashup/

'Selling the faith: the thoughts of Scott Morrison, aged 21, on building influence and growing the flock', 4 May 2021: www.crikey.com.au/2021/05/04/inq-morrison-full-university-thesis/

'The making of a mega-church and the earthly rules that keep it in financial heaven', 20 May 2021: www.crikey.com.au/2021/05/20/hillsong-brian-houston-finances/

'Houston, we have a problem: Hillsong brings in the crisis management lawyers', 31 May 2021: www.crikey.com.au/2021/05/31/hillsong-brings-in-crisis-management-lawyers/

'Hillsong calls in top "high stakes" US lawyers as indecently assaulted student calls for an end to church cover-ups', 1 June 2021: www.crikey.com.au/2021/06/01/hillsong-calls-in-finest-legal-minds/

'Sins of the father—The dark past of Australia's megachurch', 25 August 2021: www.crikey.com.au/2021/08/25/hillsong-frank-houston-brian-houston-charges/

'David Cowdrey knows how the Houstons operate—and now he's telling his story', 26 August 2021: www.crikey.com.au/2021/08/26/frank-houston-abuse-victim-story/

'Morrison does religion and politics—but you might not know where one stops and the other begins', 31 August 2021: www.crikey. com.au/2021/08/31/scott-morrison-hillsong-brian-houston-pentecostalism/

'"The Lord wants me to be prime minister"—how Scott Morrison foretold his destiny', 3 September 2021: www.crikey.com. au/2021/09/03/scott-morrison-lord-god-prime-minister/

'Brian Houston still wields soft power in Washington. What does that mean for Australia?', 12 October 2021: www.crikey.com. au/2021/10/12/brian-houstons-soft-power-in-washington/

'Bruce Baird and The Family—the PM's Christian scaffolding', 12 October 2021: www.crikey.com.au/2021/10/12/bruce-baird-the-family-pms-christian-scaffolding/

'It's time to call it out: Scott Morrison doesn't care about secular accountability', 12 October 2021: www.crikey.com.au/2021/ 10/12/its-time-to-call-it-out-scott-morrison-doesnt-care-about-secular-accountability/

'Morrison's political deeds must be seen through a godly lens', 12 October 2021: www.crikey.com.au/2021/10/12/scott-morrison-political-deeds-through-religion/

'PM and the pastor: how Morrison and Houston became Australia's religious power couple', 12 October 2021: www.crikey.com.au/ 2021/10/12/scott-morrison-brian-houston-relationship-hillsong/

'Scott Morrison "invested" $4m of public money in a Christian group. For such a time as this?', 8 February 2022: www.crikey. com.au/2022/02/08/scott-morrison-4-million-christian-esther-foundation/

'Drunk, in a woman's hotel room: revelations of Brian Houston's behaviour threaten his hold on Hillsong', 18 March 2022: 'www.crikey.com.au/2022/03/18/brian-houston-revelations-hillsong/

'"No meaningful inquiry" into rape allegations against Hillsong pastor', 23 March 2022: www.crikey.com.au/2022/03/23/ hillsong-no-meaningful-inquiry-pastor-rape-allegations/

'Houston says sorry as US pastor blows the whistle on Hillsong's business tactics', 31 March 2022: www.crikey.com.au/2022/03/31/hillsong-houston-us-pastor-blows-whistle-on-business-tactics/

'Hillsong thanks *Crikey* for our service, and promises "no more secrets"', 8 June 2022: www.crikey.com.au/2022/06/08/hillsong-thanks-crikey-promises-no-more-secrets/

'Jacob Harrison's therapy involved washing Brian Houston's car', 21 June 2022: www.crikey.com.au/2022/06/21/hillsongs-one80tc-rehab-did-his-head-in/

'Taxpayers pay for "Hillsong indoctrination centre with a mild interest in rehab"', 21 June 2022: www.crikey.com.au/2022/06/21/taxpayers-pay-for-hillsong-indoctrination-centre-with-a-mild-interest-in-rehab/

'Hillsong whistleblower: more secrets emerge from the Till on the Hill', 15 August 2022: www.crikey.com.au/2022/08/15/hillsong-whistleblower-natalie-moses-scandal/

'God's business: how the big religions scripted a massive tax handout', 11 October 2022: www.crikey.com.au/2022/10/11/sweet-charity-religion-tax-australian-catholic-bishops-conference/

'How the Coalition ignored experts to protect religious charities', 12 October 2022: www.crikey.com.au/2022/10/12/sweet-charity-coalition-ignored-experts-religious-charities/

'How allegations of rape against a Hillsong pastor led to a hunt for the leaker—and one woman being blamed', 18 October 2022: www.crikey.com.au/2022/10/18/hillsong-defence-natalie-moses-rape-allegation/

'"Fraud, money laundering and tax evasion": Wilkie tables Hillsong whistleblower documents', 9 March 2023: www.crikey.com.au/2023/03/09/andrew-wilkie-hillsong-whistleblower-documents/

Books/Journals

Hazel Houston, *Being Frank: The Frank Houston story*, Marshall Pickering, 1989

Scott John Morrison, *Religion and Society—a micro approach. An examination of the Christian Brethren Assemblies in the Sydney Metropolitan Area, 1964–1989*, University of New South Wales, 1989.

Brian Houston, *The Church I See*, 1993

Barry Chant, *The Spirit of Pentecost Origins and Development of the Pentecostal movement in Australia, 1870–1939*, PhD thesis, D.Min, Macquarie University, 1999

Brian Houston, *You Need More Money*, Brian Houston Ministries, Sydney, 1999

Shane Clifton, *Pentecostal Churches in Transition: Analysing the developing ecclesiology of the Assemblies of God in Australia*, Brill, Boston, 2009

Denise A. Austin and Shane Clifton, 'Australian Pentecostalism: from Marginalised to Megachurches', *Asia-Pacific Pentecostalism*, Vol. 31, July 2019: brill.com/display/book/9789004396708/BP000020.xml

Andrew Denton, *Kingdom Builders*, 2020

Monique Rafton, *Losing My Religion*, dissertation submitted in fulfilment of the requirement for the Master in Development Studies, Geneva, 2022

Unknown author, 'History of Lower Hutt Assemblies of God until 2013', 2022

Mark Jennings, *Happy: LGBTQ+ Experiences of Australian Pentecostal-Charismatic Christianity*, Springer, 2023

Hazel Houston, 'One Hundred Men', informal church history

Reports and official documents
Australian Charities and Not-for-profits Commission
——Kenneth Copeland Ministries Eagle Mountain International Church Ltd: www.acnc.gov.au/charity/charities/a286f520-39af-e811-a95e-000d3ad24c60/people
——Jerry Savelle Ministries International; Heritage Of Faith Christian Centre Limited: www.acnc.gov.au/charity/charities/607dc3c2-38af-e811-a962-000d3ad24a0d/people

Assemblies of God in Australia, Special Executive Meeting minutes, 22 December 1999, Sydney airport: www.childabuseroyalcommission.gov.au/sites/default/files/ACC.0001.001.0001.pdf

——Report on trip of John Lewis and Keith Ainge to New Zealand and Sydney, 28–29 November 2000: www.childabuseroyalcommission.gov.au/sites/default/files/ACC.0001.001.0004_R.pdf

Hillsong Church, Minutes of Special Elders Meeting, 29 November 2000: www.childabuseroyalcommission.gov.au/sites/default/files/HIL.0001.001.0007_R.pdf

Governor-General's Speech, Address-in-Reply, Louise Markus MP, 17 November 2004: parlinfo.aph.gov.au/parlInfo/search/display/display.w3p;query=Id:%22chamber/hansardr/2004-11-17/0065%22

'Undertakings remedy Mercy Ministries misleading conduct', Australian Competition & Consumer Commission, 16 December 2009: www.accc.gov.au/media-release/undertakings-remedy-mercy-ministries-misleading-conduct

Theresa Pattara and Sean Barnett, 'Review of Media-Based Ministries', memorandum to Senator Grassley, 6 January 2011: www.finance.senate.gov/imo/media/doc/SFC%20Staff%20Memo%20to%20Grassley%20re%20Ministries%2001-06-11%20FINAL.pdf

'Grassley Releases Review of Tax Issues Raised by Media-based Ministries', United States Senate Committee on Finance, 6 January 2011: www.finance.senate.gov/ranking-members-news/grassley-releases-review-of-tax-issues-raised-by-media-based-ministries

Royal Commission into Institutional Responses to Child Sexual Abuse, 'Report of Case study no. 18: The response of the Australian Christian Churches and affiliated Pentecostal churches to allegations of child sexual abuse', Commonwealth of Australia, 2015: www.childabuseroyalcommission.gov.au/case-studies/case-study-18-australian-christian-churches

Royal Commission into Institutional Responses to Child Sexual Abuse, Vol. 16, Final Report, Commonwealth of Australia, 2017: www.childabuseroyalcommission.gov.au/final-report

Strengthening for Purpose: Australian Charities and Not-for-profits Commission Legislative Review, 2018: treasury.gov.au/publication/p2018-t318031

'Response to *60 Minutes*', Hillsong, 20 September 2021: hillsong.com/newsroom/blog/2021/09/response-to-60-minutes/

Report of the Inquiry into the Appointment of the Former Prime Minister to Administer Multiple Departments, The Hon Virginia Bell AC, 25 November 2022: www.ministriesinquiry.gov.au

Documents presented by Mr Andrew Wilkie MP on 9 March 2023, federal parliament: www.aph.gov.au/Parliamentary_Business/Chamber_documents/Tabled_Papers/Documents_presented_by_Mr_Andrew_Wilkie_MP_on_9_March_2023

Australian Securities and Investments Commission, Current & Historical Company Extract: Shiloh Ministries Australia Ltd, 30 October 2023

Author Interviews

A large number of interviews were conducted with former Hillsong followers who did not wish to be identified. The following people have agreed to be identified:

Geoff Bullock, founding Hillsong music pastor
Pastor Bob Cotton, Maitland Christian Church
David Cowdery, victim/survivor of abuse by Frank Houston
Anna Crenshaw, Hillsong College student
Peter Fowler, victim/survivor of abuse by Frank Houston
Glen Moses, husband of Natalie Moses who took legal action against Hillsong, claiming whistleblower status
Cara Phillips, whistleblower exposing religious-based abuse at the Esther Foundation, Perth

Ted Sherwood, certified practising accountant who keeps checks
    on religious charities
Boz Tchividjian, founder of GRACE, a not-for-profit focused on
    church sex abuse